DATE DUE

Marriage and Caste in America

BOOKS BY KAY S. HYMOWITZ

Liberation's Children
Ready or Not

MARRIAGE and CASTE in AMERICA

. . . . . .

*Separate and Unequal Families
in a Post-Marital Age*

KAY S. HYMOWITZ

Ivan R. Dee

CHICAGO 2006

Most of the contents of this book appeared originally in *City Journal*, published by the Manhattan Institute.

www.ivanrdee.com

Library of Congress Cataloging-in-Publication Data:
Hymowitz, Kay S., 1948–
  Marriage and caste in America : separate and unequal families in a post-marital age / Kay S. Hymowitz.
     p. cm.
  Includes index.
  ISBN-13: 978-1-56663-709-1 (cloth : alk. paper)
  ISBN-10: 1-56663-709-0 (cloth : alk. paper)
  1. Marriage—United States. 2. Social classes—United States. 3. United States—Social conditions—21st century. I. Title.
  HQ536.H96 2006
  306.81086'20973—dc22

                                                        2006016028

To my parents, Leon and Emily Sunstein,
who know a thing or two about marriage

Acknowledgments

I WANT TO THANK both the William E. Simon Foundation and the Randolph Foundation, which generously provided funding for my work at *City Journal*. Brian Anderson was an enormous help in updating the essays and shaping them into a coherent argument. Myron Magnet was, as usual, a wonderful combination of delighted booster and demanding taskmaster. At the Manhattan Institute, Larry Mone, Lindsay Young Craig, Clarice Smith, Ed Craig, Ben Plotinsky, David DesRosiers, and Molly Harsh provided much needed support.

I owe a great debt to Peter Cove who came to me with an idea for a book about "missing men" several years ago. This book is not the one Peter had in mind or that I ever expected to write, but his idea inspired much of my recent work for *City Journal* and helped bring some of my previously published articles into a new light. Thanks also to Lee Bowes, Jan Rosenthal, Fred Siegel, Larry Mead, Ron Haskins, Sara McLanahan, Andrea Kane, Sara Brown, and Emily Flint. By giving me the opportunity to review relevant books that might otherwise have escaped my attention, and by insisting that I carefully recount the arguments of those books, the guys at *Commentary*—Gary Rosen, Neil Kozodoy, and Gabe

Acknowledgments

Schoenfeld—unwittingly aided and abetted these essays. I am grateful to the many researchers too numerous to mention here who took the time to explain their work to me; I thank them also for declining to comment on my obvious innumeracy during those conversations. I also want to thank the men and women I probed about marriage and parenthood at America Works, in hospitals, in postnatal clinics, and, even on occasion, on the streets of Brooklyn.

Thanks, yet again, to my youngest child, Anna, who has reached the last year of suffering through my deadlines and obsessions as she heads off to college, and, of course, to my husband Paul Hymowitz, whose humor has lightened many loads.

K. S. H.

New York City
July 2006

Contents

Marriage and Caste in America

Introduction

MY ARGUMENT IN these essays can easily be summed up: the breakdown of marriage in the United States—which began about forty years ago as divorce and out-of-wedlock birthrates started to soar—threatens America's future. It is turning us into a nation of separate and unequal families.

Sounds overwrought? Bear with me, for I offer this bleak warning not out of religious conviction—I am an agnostic—nor out of any devotion to Eisenhower-era family life—I was around then and know better—nor because of a Hallmark tenderness for the institution—I've been married too long for that. I say it because it has become clear that family breakdown lies at the heart of our nation's most obstinate social problems, especially poverty and inequality. To put it more broadly, there is no way to attack these worrisome economic trends without tackling culture—the system of beliefs, values, and practices that help us define and live a good life.

Most people assume that divorce, unmarried motherhood, fatherlessness, and custody battles are all equal-opportunity domestic misfortunes, affecting the denizens of West Virginia trailer parks or Bronx housing projects just as they do those of Malibu beach homes or Park Avenue co-ops. It's understandable that this conviction is wide-spread; the media loves stories of celebrities and billionaires gone wild. Nevertheless, as I explain in detail in the title essay to this book, the assumption that Americans are all in the same boat when it comes to marriage collapse is dead wrong.

There *is* a typical single mother, and she is not Murphy Brown or Angelina Jolie. (It's necessary to begin by talking about mothers because in the vast majority of cases it is women who have custody of their children.) She is poor, or near poor. She has no college degree. She has few of the skills essential for negotiating a tough new economy. On the other side of the tracks is her college-educated counterpart. She is skilled, of course. She is also married. Now add this fact to the mix: children of single mothers are less successful on just about every measure than children growing up with their married parents regardless of their income, race, or education levels: they are more prone to drug and alcohol abuse, to crime, and to school failure; they are less likely to graduate from college; they are more likely to have children at a young age, and more likely to do so when they are unmarried. Put the two trends together—more marriage among the better educated, on the one hand, and diminished prospects for the children of single mothers on the other—and you get double trouble for the country's most vulnerable: poor or working-class single mothers with little education having children who will grow up to be low-income single mothers and fathers with little education who will have children who will become low-income single parents—and so forth. Meanwhile college-educated, middle-class married mothers are raising children who go to college, get married, and only then have children—who will grow up and go to college, get married, and so on. A self-perpetuating single-mother proletariat on the one hand, and a self-perpetuating, comfortable middle class on the other. Not exactly what America should look like, is it?

At this point, inquiring minds want to know the answers to several questions. Why are low-income mothers not getting hitched before they have kids while middle-class women are? And why does marriage make such a big difference to children—and to their future status—anyway? Is it just that two parents mean more "economic and social inputs," as social scientists might put it?

The answer to the latter question is a categorical no, and to understand why, we need to step back for a moment and think about what marriage is. Marriage exists in every known society, no matter how poor or rich; it is what social scientists call a "human universal." But marriage, it is obvious, also comes in various shapes and sizes. That is, in addition to being a universal, it is also a cultural institution with specific cultural meanings that have been shaped by local history, economy, religion, and social ideals. American marriage is no exception.

It may seem odd to talk about American marriage given the unruly diversity of the population, but there is such a thing and it is the subject of Chapter 2, "What American Marriage Does." Americans in the early days of the republic consciously set out to define their unions in opposition to the arranged, patriarchal mergers of old Europe. American marriage was to be in keeping with the country's founding ideals—freedom, self-government, and individualism. Instead of the extended kinship systems common elsewhere, American couples were supposed to be breaking their own sod and setting up independent households on

Midwestern prairies and in New England towns, where they would raise the next generation of self-governing citizens. While the next centuries saw notable changes in American marital law—wives gradually escaped their husbands' absolute legal authority, and blacks earned the full marriage rights denied them since slavery—the basic blueprint remained: a freely choosing, self-governing, economically independent couple grooming children to become free, self-governing, economically independent adults.

That is, until the late 1960s. The sexual revolution and feminist movement of that era changed American society in myriad ways, but what interests us here is their profound effect on marriage. For the first time in history—not just American history but the history of known human society— people began to toy with the idea that children and marriage were really two discrete life phenomena. If they wanted, if it made them happy, why shouldn't men and women have children without being married? To be sure, this rupture between marriage and child-rearing was unfolding in Western Europe as well, but given how much Americans relied on individual families to pass on cultural ideals, the unmarriage revolution in the United States held special dangers. The founders had imagined independent nuclear couples not just as pursuing happiness but as performing a vital social task: raising their children to thrive in a country that valued freedom and self-government above all. That ideal was thrown in the discard pile, and, wonder of wonders, the percentage of children growing up in single-parent homes skyrocketed and child poverty began to rise.

The unmarriage revolution hit African Americans especially hard, as I show in Chapter 3. In 1965 a little-known assistant secretary of labor named Daniel Patrick Moynihan warned of a growing crisis in the black ghetto, where a full quarter of children were being born to unmarried women. Today in some cities it is upward of 80 percent. There are a variety of reasons for the vulnerability of blacks to the marital sea change of the second half of the twentieth century, including the legacy of slavery and an accommodating welfare system that made it possible for poor women and their children to get by. But a battalion of academics, civil rights leaders, and feminists also actively fomented the revolutionary doctrine. These groups accused Moynihan of racism and—ignoring the fact that until 1960 the vast majority of black children had been born to married couples—celebrated the strong and independent African-American woman and her robust kinship groups. The nuclear family, they scoffed, was nothing worth imitating. It was really just a white thing.

From the vantage point of the present, what is astonishing is how few people stopped to consider what unmarriage meant for children. As marriage was redefined as a state-stamped intimate relationship between two adults, children were relegated to the incidental; they were an add-on, like dessert, rather than the main course. Throughout the 1970s and '80s, even as single motherhood and child poverty rose, social scientists studying the family rarely paid attention to marital status. The legal system was also remarkably nonchalant. The courts began treating marriage as a civil contract between two consenting adults, not so different from a mortgage agreement, and in child-custody disputes they increasingly ignored distinctions between married and unmarried parents.

What makes this oversight all the more surprising is that from early on American marriage had been exceptionally child-centered, a custom that raised the eyebrows of foreign observers from the days of the young republic—as it still does today. In fact there are good social and economic reasons for the American tendency toward diligent parenting. Educating the young for a democratic society and a modern, changing economy—what I call in Chapter 4 "The Mission"—has always been a big undertaking. Early-nineteenth-century child experts began recommending that parents encourage their child's self-development and free exploration, or what we might call these days their cognitive and emotional development. Clearly Americans have not always pursued The Mission with the zeal of today's soccer parents. You can be sure that the mothers on depression-era Kansas farms didn't play Beethoven for their six-month-olds or spend their weekends screaming on the sidelines of soccer games. But of course these parents had the advantage of not having to worry about preparing their kids for an age of global competition.

For adding to children's woes wrought by the unmarriage revolution was the unfortunate fact of its timing. During the same decades that American marriage was undergoing deconstruction, the economy was moving into an increasingly competitive postindustrial age. Manufacturing jobs that once allowed high school dropouts to support a family disappeared; to make sure that your kids were comfortably middle class, you now had to see to it they went to college. Yet the very system that best sustained children on the way to State U—that is, American marriage with its implied Mission—was under attack. It is possible for low-income mothers to undertake The Mission without husbands, and many do. But it is much harder and much more rare. Observers find that low-income single mothers are more likely to think of their children's development as unfolding naturally. Insofar as their kids need educating, they assume, teachers will take care of it. Meanwhile their middle-class counterparts are strategizing their children's growth the way the generals planned D-day. Naturally they're going to make sure they have enlisted men—husbands, in other words—to help them in such a massive campaign.

Yet despite a great economic transformation that was making two parents crucial for children to get ahead, Americans remained rather blasé about the role of men in the family. Men might be on hand to help raise their kids; then again, they might not. If anyone worried whether losing one of their principal social roles would hurt men, we didn't hear much about it—a considerable omission in revolutionary planning. As I show in "Dads in the 'Hood," for the men who grow up where marriage is all but extinct, as it is in the inner city, the consequences of the unmarriage revolution have been especially tragic. Having gone through childhood dadless themselves, they are often determined to "step up" and be responsible. But they have no cultural model either of fatherhood or of a constructive partnership with their children's mother. No surprise there: no culture has ever designed a model of fatherhood without matrimony. With the connection between marriage and children totally severed, dads in the 'hood often have children by several different women who themselves may have sons and daughters by different men. The end result is a maelstrom of confusion, jealousy, rage, abandonment, and violence.

But perhaps the most damaging consequence of unmarriage for young men—and women as well, as I show in "The Teen Mommy Track"—is the loss of the life script that would allow them to escape the struggles of poverty. Every society has a life script—though most people grasp it in only the most subliminal way—that suits its particular economy and culture. In the United States the script has a number of acts: childhood, adolescence and schooling—or apprenticeship or some other preparation for work that would lead to self-sufficiency—then marriage, and only then children. Middle-class children growing up in today's information economy know that the preparation act of this script will last well into their twenties and possibly even thirties; that is why the average age of marriage has climbed in recent decades. But low-income children of single mothers are actors in a different, far more chaotic, drama. Without a culturally endorsed script, there is no planning for the future, no deliberate decision-making, no ambitions, and few dreams. In the middle-class model you prepare for marriage by becoming self-sufficient and looking for the right partner to share a home and children. For many low-income young people, education is neither here nor there, and sex simply happens. Then babies happen. In fact, life happens. And so does poverty.

Skeptics often scoff at marriage proponents like myself; everyone should choose to live as he or she pleases, they say, a position that makes gay marriage seem a no-brainer. The story of the unmarriage revolution shows that stance to be, to say the least, problematic. Marriage is not a lifestyle choice, a bundle of benefits, or a piece of paper. And it goes far beyond planning a wedding and applying for a home mortgage. As *the* core cultural institution, marriage orders life in ways we only dimly understand. It carries with it signals about how we should live, signals that are in line with both our economy and our politics in the largest sense. In choosing their own spouses and planning their own home lives, people act out the individual freedom and the pursuit of happiness that are our primary values. In waiting to marry until they are capable of financial independence, and in devoting themselves to their children's social, emotional, and cognitive development, a couple passes on the ideals of self-sufficiency and individual initiative to the next generation. When the poor lost the language of American marriage, they lost a great deal more than a spouse. They lost touch with the values of self-sufficiency and individual ambition. They lost a life script. They lost the rules of The Mission. And they lost the language of opportunity.

This sounds pretty grim, I know. But my final chapters, "The End of Herstory" and "It's Morning After in America," offer reason for hope. Especially in a young and dynamic society like our own, culture can change, and so can attitudes toward marriage. By the later 1990s young middle-class men and women were clearly turning their backs on the unmarriage revolution that had shaped their own childhoods. In surveys they pronounced themselves passionate fans of the institution. They began to spend their time watching shows like *The Bachelor* and planning weddings that rivaled that of Princess Di. They announced their preference for large families. Young mothers soured on feminist careerism, became Mrs. Somebody, and, dissatisfied with the idea of a full-time day-care and latchkey childhood, put their energies into figuring out ways to spend more time with their children. A rising number even quit their jobs. Now, instead of an unmarriage revolution we have an "opt-out revolution." In fact what we are seeing is a generation of hyper-parents; they are surely the most passionate Missionaries the country has ever produced.

There are several reasons for this—a big jump in the numbers of young immigrants, which is a population that tends to be relatively traditional on sex and marriage issues, and an information economy that requires intensive parenting. But the biggest cause behind the waning of the unmarriage revolution is simply generational backlash. Generation X and its younger brothers and sisters looked into the unmarriage abyss and decided they didn't want to go there. The question that confronts us now is whether the poor and near-poor can do the same. It will take a counter-revolution, but, as you'll see in many of the following essays, stranger things have happened.

When we use the word marriage in everyday conversation, we know what we mean: the (hopefully) permanent union, based on love, of a man and a woman—or, depending on your position on gay marriage, of two adults. The first two essays in this book ask readers to put aside that everyday definition—what we might call "Marriage: The Personal Relationship"—to get at what social scientists mean when they refer to marriage as a foundation of society—that is, "Marriage: The Institution."

"Marriage: The Personal Relationship" concerns two people. It evokes love, commitment, vows, celebrations, honeymoons, and couples therapists. But "Marriage: The Institution" refers to an arrangement with a profound collective purpose. As a social institution, marriage helps organize social life. As a social institution, it contains complex messages about what we value and how we should live. As a social institution, it serves vital social ends; in particular, it organizes the rearing of the next generation. Every society has had to deal with the problem of the long and total dependence of the human infant; every society has answered that problem with some form of the institution we call marriage.

Beginning in the mid-1960s Americans decided to separate the institution from its primary function. With the normalization of divorce and unwed childbearing, they effectively agreed that children and marriage were ready to go their separate ways, that rather than being chiefly about

*children, wedlock would be mostly about adult happiness.
But it turns out that just as it's not nice to fool Mother
Nature, so it's a mistake to trick a bulwark social
institution. Separating the institution and its primary
purpose has predictably harmed children; it has also
undermined the nation's ability to live up to its promise as
the country bisects into separate and unequal families.*

1

Marriage and Caste

For a while it looked like Hurricane Katrina would accomplish what the NAACP never could: reviving civil rights liberalism as a major force in American politics. There it was for the whole world to see: the United States was two nations, one rich, one poor and largely black, one driving away in the family SUV to sleep in the snug guest rooms of suburban friends and relatives, the other sunk in the fetid misery of the Superdome. *Newsweek*, echoing Michael Harrington's 1962 landmark book that ignited the War on Poverty, titled its Katrina coverage "The Other America" and warned the nation not to return to the "old evasions, hypocrisies, and not-so-benign neglect" of the "problems of poverty, race, and class."

Although that revival of liberalism lasted only about five minutes, the post-Katrina insight was correct. There *are* millions of poor Americans, living not just in down-on-your-luck hardship but in entrenched, multigenerational poverty. There is growing inequality between the haves and the have-nots. And there are reasons to worry whether the American dream is within reach of all.

But what two-America talk doesn't get is just how much these ominous trends are entangled with the collapse of the nuclear family. While Americans have been squabbling about gay marriage, they have managed to miss the real marriage-and-social-justice issue, one that affects far more citizens and threatens to undermine the American project. We are now a nation of separate and unequal families, not only living separate and unequal lives but, more worrisome, destined for separate and unequal futures.

Two-America Jeremiahs usually nod at the single-parent family as a piece of the inequality story, then quickly change the subject to describe—accurately, as far as it goes—an economy that has implacably squeezed out manufacturing jobs, reduced wages for the low-skilled, and made a wallet-busting college education crucial to a middle-class future. But one can't disentangle the economic from the family piece. Given that families socialize children for success—or not—and given how marriage orders lives, they are the same problem. Separate and unequal families produce separate and unequal economic fates.

Most people understand what happened to the American family over the last half-century along these lines: the birth control pill begat the sexual and feminist revolutions of the 1960s, which begat the decline of the traditional nuclear family, which in turn introduced the country to a major new demographic: the single mother. Divorce became as ubiquitous as the automobile; half of all marriages, we are often reminded, will end in family court. Growing financial independence and changing mores not only gave women the freedom to divorce in lemminglike numbers; it also allowed them to dispense with marriage altogether and have children, Murphy Brown style, on their own. (This is leaving aside inner-city teenage mothers, whom just about everyone sees as an entirely different and more troubling category.) Today, we frequently hear, a third of all children are born to unmarried women.

To put it a little differently, after the 1960s women no longer felt compelled to follow the life course charted in a once-popular childhood rhyme—first comes love, then marriage, then the baby carriage. Sure, some people got married, had kids, and stayed married for life, but the hegemony of Ozzie and his brood was past. Alternative families are just the way things are; for better or for worse, in a free society people get to choose their own "lifestyles"—bringing their children along for the ride—and they are doing so not just in the United States but all over the Western world.

That picture turns out to be as equivocal as an Escher lithograph, however. As the massive social upheaval following the 1960s—what Francis Fukuyama has termed "the Great Disruption"—has settled into the new normal, social scientists are finding that when it comes to the family, America really has become two nations. The old-fashioned married-couple-with-children model is doing quite well among college-educated women. It is primarily among lower-income women with only a high school education that it is in poor health. This fact may not conform to the view from Hollywood; movies from *Kramer vs. Kramer* to *The Ice Storm* to *The Squid and the Whale*, not to mention unmarried celebrity moms like Goldie Hawn and Katie Holmes, have helped reinforce the perception that elite women snubbing a conformist patriarchy have been the vanguard of a vast social change. Now it's pretty clear that this is a myth saying more about La-La Land than the reality of American family breakdown.

The most important recent analysis of that reality is "The Uneven Spread of Single-Parent Families," a 2004 paper by Harvard's David Ellwood and Christopher Jencks. The Kennedy School profs divide American mothers into three categories by education level: women with a college degree or higher; women with a high school diploma (including those with some college, whose trends look very similar to those with high school alone); and women who never graduated high school. The paper's findings are worth pondering in some detail.

Forty-five years ago there was only a small difference in the way American women went about the whole marriage-and-children question. Just about everyone, from a Smith grad living in New Canaan, Connecticut, to a high school dropout in Appalachia, first tied the knot and only then delivered the bouncing bundle of joy. As of 1960 the percentage of women with either a college or high school diploma who had children without first getting married was so low that you'd need a magnifying glass to find it on a graph; even the percentage of high school dropouts who were never-married mothers barely hit 1 percent. Moreover, after getting married and having a baby, almost all women stayed married. A little under 5 percent of mothers in the top third of the education distribution and about 6 percent of the middle group were either divorced or separated (though these figures don't include divorced-and-then-remarried mothers). And while marital breakup was higher among mothers who were high school dropouts, their divorce rate was still only a modest 8 percent or so.

That all changed in the decades following the 1960s, when, as everyone who was alive at the time remembers, the American family appeared to be on the verge of self-immolation. For women, marriage and children no longer seemed part of the same story line. Instead of staying married for the kids, mothers at every education level joined the national divorce binge. By 1980 the percentage of divorced college-educated mothers had more than doubled, to 12 percent—about the same percentage as divorced mothers with a high school diploma or with some college. For high school dropout mothers, the percentage increased to 15 percent. More women had children without getting married at all. So far the story conforms to general theory.

But around 1980 the family-forming habits of college grads and uneducated women went their separate ways. For the next decade the proportion of college-educated moms filing for divorce stopped increasing, and by 1990 it actually began falling. This was not the case for the least-educated mothers, who continued on a divorce spree for another ten years. It was only in 1990 that their increase in divorce also started to slow and by 2000 to decline, though it was too late to close the considerable gap between them and their more privileged sisters.

Far more dramatic were the divergent trends in what was still known at the time as illegitimacy. Yes, out-of-wedlock childbearing among women with college diplomas tripled, but because their numbers started at Virtually Nonexistent in 1960 (a fraction of 1 percent), they moved up only to Minuscule in 1980 (a little under 3 percent of mothers in the top third of education distribution) to end up at a Rare 4 percent.

Things were radically different for mothers in the lower two educational levels. They decided that marriage and children were two entirely unconnected life experiences. That decline in their divorce rate after 1990? Well, it turns out the reason for it wasn't that these women had thought better of putting their children through a parental breakup, as many of their more educated sisters had; it was that they weren't getting married in the first place. Throughout the 1980s and '90s, the out-of-wedlock birthrate soared to about 15 percent among mothers with less than a high school education and 10 percent of those with a high school diploma or with some college.

Many people assume that these low-income never-married mothers are teen mothers, but teens are only a subset of unmarried mothers, and an increasingly small one in recent years. Yes, the United States continues to be the teen-mommy capital of the Western world, with 4 percent of teen girls having babies, a rate considerably higher than Europe's. But that rate is almost one-third lower than it was in 1991, and according to up-to-the-minute figures from the National Center for Health Statistics, teens account for only about a quarter of unwed births—compared with half in 1970. Today 55 percent of unmarried births are to women between twenty and twenty-four; another 28 percent are to twenty-five- to twenty-nine-year-olds. These days it is largely low-income twentysomethings who are having a baby without a wedding ring. The good news is that single mothers are not as likely to be fifteen; the bad news is that there is now considerable evidence to suggest that, while their prospects may be a little better than their teenage sisters' would be, they are not dramatically so.

Race has also added to misperceptions about single mothers. It's easy to see why, with close to 70 percent of black children born to single mothers today—including educated mothers—compared with 25 percent of nonblack kids. But blacks make up only 12 percent of the country's population, and black children account for only one-third of the nation's out-of-wedlock kids.

Tune out the static from teen pregnancy, race, and Murphy Brown, then, and the big news comes into focus: starting in 1980, Americans began to experience a widening Marriage Gap that has reached dangerous proportions. As of 2000 only about 10 percent of mothers with sixteen or more years of education—that is, with a college degree or higher—were living without husbands. Compare that with 36 percent of mothers who have between nine and fourteen years of education. All the statistics about marriage so often rehashed in magazine and newspaper articles hide a startling truth. Yes, 33 percent of children are born to single mothers; in 2004, according to the National Center for Health Statistics, that amounted to 1.5 million children, the highest number ever. But the vast majority of those children are going home from the maternity wards to low-rent apartments. Yes, experts predict that about 40 to 50 percent of marriages will break up. But most of those divorces will involve women who have always shopped at Wal-Mart. "[T]he rise in single-parent families is concentrated among blacks and among the less educated," summarize Ellwood and Jencks. "It hardly occurred at all among women with a college degree."

When Americans began their family revolution four decades ago, they didn't talk much about its effect on children. That oversight now haunts the country as it becomes increasingly clear that the Marriage Gap results in a yawning social divide. If you want to discuss why childhood poverty numbers have remained stubbornly high through the years when the nation was aggressively trying to lower them, begin with the Marriage Gap. Thirty-six percent of female-headed families are below the poverty line. Compare that with 6 percent of married-couple families in poverty—a good portion of whom are recent low-skilled immigrants, whose poverty, if history is any guide, is temporary. The same goes if you want to analyze the inequality problem— start with the Marriage Gap. Virtually all—92 percent—of children whose families make over $75,000 a year are living with both parents. On the other end of the income scale, the situation is reversed: only about 20 percent of kids in families earning under $15,000 live with both parents.

Princeton sociologist Sara McLanahan, co-author of the breakthrough book *Growing Up with a Single Parent*, has fleshed out the implications of the Marriage Gap for children in an important paper in *Demography*—and they're not pretty. McLanahan observes that after 1970 women at all income levels began to marry at older ages, and the average age of first marriage moved into the mid-twenties. But where mothers at the top of the income scale also put off having children until they were married, spending their years before marriage getting degrees or working, those at the bottom did neither.

The results radically split the experiences of children. Children in the top quartile now have mothers who not only are likely to be married but also are older, more mature, better educated, and nearly three times as likely to be employed (whether full- or part-time) as are mothers of children in the bottom quartile. And not only do top-quartile children have what are likely to be more effective mothers; they also get the benefit of more time and money from their live-in fathers.

For children born at the bottom of the income scale, the situation is the reverse. They face a *decrease* in what McLanahan terms "resources": their mothers are younger, less stable, less educated, and, of course, have less money. Adding to their woes, those children aren't getting much (or any) financial support and time from their fathers. Surprisingly, McLanahan finds that in Europe too—where welfare supports for "lone parents," as they are known in Britain, are much higher than in the United States—single mothers are still more likely to be poor and less educated. As in the United States, so in Europe and, no doubt, the rest of the world: children in single-parent families are getting less of just about everything that we know helps to lead to successful adulthood.

All this makes depressing sense, but when you think about it the Marriage Gap itself presents a puzzle. Why would women working for a pittance at supermarket cash registers decide to have children without getting married while women writing briefs at Debevoise & Plimpton, who could easily afford to go it alone, insist on finding husbands before they start families? For a long time social scientists assumed, reasonably enough, that economic self-sufficiency would lead more women to choose single motherhood. And to listen to the drone of complaint about men around water coolers, in Internet chat rooms, on the Oxygen Network, and in Maureen Dowdworld, there would seem to be plenty of potential recruits for Murphy Browndom. Certainly when they talk to pollsters, women say they don't think there's anything *wrong* with having a baby without a husband. Yet the women who are forgoing husbands are precisely the ones who can least afford to do so.

The conventional answer to the puzzle is this: in an economy marked by manufacturing decline, especially in cities, too many of the potential husbands for low-income women are either flipping burgers, unemployed, or in jail— in other words, poor marriage material. But three facts raise doubts about this theory.

One, it's not just unemployed men or McDonald's cooks who have become marriage-avoidant; working-class men with decent jobs are also shying from the altar. Two, cohabitation among low-income couples has been increasing; about 40 percent of all out-of-wedlock babies today are born to cohabiting parents. Why would there be a dearth of marriageable men when there appear to be plenty of cohabitable fathers? And three, marriage improves the economic situation of low-income women, even if their husbands are only deliverymen or janitors. In a large and highly regarded study, the Urban Institute's Robert Lerman concluded that married, low-income, low-educated women enjoyed significantly higher living standards than comparable single mothers. Joe Sixpack may not be Mr. Darcy, but financially, at any rate, he's a lot better than no husband at all.

Still, whatever the arguments against it, the no-marriageable-men theory is entrenched in policy circles and in the academy and is unlikely to go anywhere soon, so let's try another approach to the Marriage Gap conundrum. Instead of asking why poor and near-poor women have stopped marrying before having children, let's think instead about why educated women continue to do so—even though, in order to be accepted in polite company or to put food on the table, they don't need to.

Marriage and Caste

One possible answer is especially pertinent to the Marriage Gap: educated women know they'd better marry if they want their children to succeed academically, which increasingly is critical to succeeding in the labor market. The New Economy may have made single motherhood a workable arrangement for high-earning mothers in purely economic terms, but it made a husband a must-have in terms of child-rearing. No one understands better than an Amherst or Stanford B.A. that her children will have to go to college one day—the bigger the college name, the better—if they are to keep their middle-class status. These women also understand how to get their kids college-bound. Educated middle-class mothers tend to be dedicated to The Mission—the careful nurturing of their children's cognitive, emotional, and social development, which, if all goes according to plan, will lead to the honor roll and a spot on the high school debate team, which will in turn lead to a good college, then perhaps a graduate or professional degree, which will all lead eventually to a fulfilling career, a big house in a posh suburb, and a sense of meaningful accomplishment.

It's common sense, backed up by plenty of research, that you'll have a better chance of fully "developing" your children—that is, of fulfilling The Mission—if you have a husband around. Children of single mothers have lower grades and educational attainment than kids who grow up with married parents, even after controlling for race, family background, and IQ. Children of divorce are also less likely to graduate and attend college, and when they do go for a B.A., they tend to go to less elite schools. Cornell professor Jennifer Gerner was baffled some years ago when she noticed that only about 10 percent of her students came from divorced families. She and her colleague Dean

Lillard examined the records of students at the nation's top fifty schools and, much to their surprise, found a similar pattern. Children who did not grow up with their two biological parents, they concluded when they published their findings, were only half as likely to go to a selective college. As adults they also earned less and had lower occupational status.

To repeat the question: Why do educated women marry before they have children? Because, like high-status women since status began, they are preparing their offspring to carry on their way of life. Marriage radically increases their chances of doing that.

This all points to a deeply worrying conclusion: the Marriage Gap—and the inequality to which it is tied—is self-perpetuating. A low-income single mother, unprepared to carry out The Mission, is more likely to raise children who will become low-income single parents, who will pass that legacy on to their children, and so on down the line. Married parents are more likely to be visiting their married children and their grandchildren in their comfortable suburban homes, and those married children will in turn be sending their offspring off to good colleges, superior jobs, and wedding parties. Instead of an opportunity-rich country for all, the Marriage Gap threatens us with a rigid caste society.

So what is it about the nuclear family that makes it work so well for children, decades after Americans have declared it optional? The economists and sociologists who study these things often answer that question with some variation of what might be called the strength-in-numbers theory. Kids with two parents are more likely to have two incomes cushioning them during their developing years. More money means more stability, less stress, better day care and health care, more books, more travel, and, most of all, a home in a good school district—all of which leads to educational and, eventually, workplace success. A husband and wife can support each other if one is laid off or if the other wants retraining or more education. They can take turns caring for the children. Or if they can afford to, they can specialize: the woman (yes, it's still almost always the woman) can take over as homework helper and soccer-team and church-group chauffeur while the man earns a salary. According to the strength-in-numbers theory, then, two parents are better than one much the way two hands are better than one: they can accomplish more.

But this theory finally doesn't explain all that much. If two parents are what make a difference, then why, when a divorced mother remarries, do her children's outcomes resemble those of children from single-parent homes more than they do those from intact families? Why do they have, on average, lower school grades, more behavior problems, and lower levels of psychological well-being—even when a stepparent improves their economic standard of living?

You could posit that children in stepfamilies may well have suffered through their parents' divorce or have had a difficult spell in a single-parent home. But what, then, do we make of cohabiting parents? Two cohabiting parents also provide few of the benefits for kids that married couples do. The Urban Institute's Robert Lerman has found that even when cohabiters resemble married couples in terms of education, number of children, and income, they experience more material hardship—things like an empty pantry or no phone or an electricity shutoff—and get less help from extended families when they do. And poverty rates of cohabiting-couple parents are double those of married couples, even controlling for education, immigration status, and race.

Others take an alternative approach to the question of why children growing up with their own two married parents do better than children growing up without their fathers. It's not marriage that makes the difference for kids, they argue; it's the kind of people who marry. Mothers who marry and stay married already have the psychological endowment that makes them both more effective partners and more competent parents. After all, we've already seen that married mothers are more likely to be educated and working than single mothers; it makes sense that whatever abilities allowed them to write their Economics 101 papers or impress a prospective boss or husband also make them successful wives and mothers. Many low-income mothers may not have the skills—or, some would argue, the IQ—that would get them their B.A. or a good job, and this deficit makes them less likely both to marry or stay married and to raise successful children. "Parents with limited cultural and material resources are unlikely to remain together in a stable marriage," Frank Furstenberg, a famed family researcher, has written in *Dissent*. "Because the possession of such psychological, human and material capital is highly related to marital stability, it is easy to confuse the effects of stable marriage with the effects of competent parenting."

The problem with this theory is that it merely tiptoes up to the obvious. There is something fundamentally different about low-income single mothers and their educated married sisters. But a key part of that difference is that educated women *still believe in marriage as an institution for raising children*. What is missing in all the ocean of research related to the Marriage Gap is any recognition that this assumption is itself an invaluable piece of cultural and psychological capital—and not just because it makes it more likely that children will grow up with a dad in the house. As society's bulwark social institution, traditional marriage—that is, childbearing within marriage—orders social life in ways that we only dimly understand.

For one thing, women who grow up in a marriage-before-children culture organize their lives around a meaningful and beneficial life script. Traditional marriage gives young people a map of life that takes them step by step from childhood to adolescence to college or other work training—which might well include postgraduate education—to the workplace, to marriage, and only then to childbearing. A marriage orientation also requires a young woman to consider the question of what man will become her husband and the father of her children as a major, if not *the* major, decision of her life. In other words, a marriage orientation demands that a woman keep her eye on the future, that she go through life with deliberation, and that she use self-discipline—especially when it comes to sex: bourgeois women still consider premature pregnancy a disaster. In short, a marriage orientation—not just marriage itself—is part and parcel of her bourgeois ambition.

When Americans announced that marriage before childbearing was optional, low-income women didn't merely lose a steadfast partner, a second income, or a trusted baby-sitter, as the strength-in-numbers theory would have it. They lost a traditional arrangement that reinforced precisely the qualities that they—and their men; let's not forget the men!—needed for upward mobility, qualities all the more important in a tough new knowledge economy. The timing could hardly have been worse. At a time when education was becoming crucial to middle-class status, the disadvantaged lost a reliable life script, a way of organizing their early lives that would prize education and culminate in childbearing only after job training and marriage. They lost one of their few institutional supports for planning ahead and taking control of their lives.

Worst of all, when Americans made marriage optional, low-income women lost a culture that told them the truth about what was best for their children. A number of researchers argue that, in fact, low-income women really do want to marry. They have "white picket dreams," say Kathryn Edin and Maria Kefalas in *Promises I Can Keep: Why Poor Women Put Motherhood Before Marriage*, and though the men in their lives cannot turn those dreams into reality, they continue to gaze longingly into the distance at marriage as a symbol of middle-class stability and comfort. What they don't have, however, is a clue about the very fact that orders the lives of their more fortunate peers: marriage and childbearing belong together. The result is separate and unequal families, now and as far as the eye can see.

As family experts find themselves surrendering to their own research and arguing more and more that marriage is central to the overall well-being of children, they often caution that it is not a cure-all. "Is Marriage a Panacea?" is the illustrative title of a 2003 article in the scholarly journal *Social Problems*, and you know the answer to the question without reading a page. No, shrinking the Marriage Gap may not be a magic potion for ending poverty or inequality or any other social problem. But it's hard to see how our two Americas can become one without more low-income men and women making their way to the altar.

Marriage may not be a panacea. But it is a *sine qua non*.

2

What American Marriage Does

These days everyone has a strong opinion about marriage, but no one seems to be sure what it is, exactly. Is it a sacramental union? Is it a public recognition of a committed love relationship? Is it a state scheme for distributing health insurance and tax breaks? Or, given what two eminent anthropologists writing in support of gay marriage in the *Washington Post* describe as a "startling diversity of socially approved forms of marriage," is the institution too varied to fit into a single, dictionary-neat meaning?

The anthropologists are right about one thing: human beings have come up with almost as many ways of getting hitched as they have languages to tell mother-in-law jokes. Some cultures allow only monogamous marriage; some accept polygamy. In many cultures the wife moves into her husband's family's home; in others the husband moves into the wife's; in still others they get a mortgage and move into their own two-bedroom ranch in Levittown. Although most cultures give husbands the primary responsibility for providing for the children, some make the wife's brother—the baby's uncle—responsible for providing the food and the bow-and-arrow lessons. Some cultures don't allow divorce;

some allow divorce but not remarriage; some allow divorce if husbands fork over most of their life savings to the likes of Raoul Felder; and others let a guy say "I divorce you" three times before booting his wife out the door.

This protean diversity is central to today's marriage debate. If marriage is, as these examples suggest, an eminently malleable social construct, why shouldn't society shape it any way it likes, especially by letting gays marry each other?

But beneath all the diversity, marriage has always had a fundamental, universal core that makes gay marriage a non sequitur: it has always governed property and inheritance rights; it has always been the means of establishing paternity, legitimacy, and the rights and responsibilities of parenthood; and because these goals involve bearing and raising children, it has always involved (at least one) man and woman. What's more, among the "startling diversity" of variations that different cultures have elaborated on this fundamental core, our own culture has produced a specifically American ideal of marriage that is inseparable from our vision of free citizenship and is deeply embedded in our history, politics, economics, and culture. Advocates for gay marriage cite the historical evolution of that ideal—which we might call republican marriage—to bolster their case, arguing that gay unions are a natural extension of America's dedication to civil rights and individual freedom. But a look at that history is enough to cast serious doubt on the advocates' case.

Strange as it seems, America's founding thinkers were as interested in the subject of marriage as any of Fox TV's bachelorettes. Given the political experiment they were designing, they had good reason, for they understood the basic sociological truth that familial relations both echo and shape the political order. "To the institution of marriage the true origin of society must be traced," James Wilson, a member of the Continental Congress and later a Supreme Court justice, wrote in 1790. Before the Revolutionary War, legal philosophers and statesmen like Wilson filled magazines and speeches with discussions of what kind of marriage would best live up to the principles of the new country. It's not surprising that they zeroed in on one quality in particular: self-government.

The founders did not sketch their ideas about marriage on a blank slate, of course. They brought to their task a set of traditional Western assumptions about the institution, and these assumptions remained implicit in their new ideal and still resurface in our current discussions. Given that marriage was originally a religious sacrament, the founders understood that the institution retained, even in their secular republic, an element of spirituality, an assertion that man is something higher than the beasts and more than a merely material being. The ceremony confers a special, human dignity upon our relations. In addition, they understood that marriage is a contract, regulated by the laws and ultimately enforceable by the state, that spells out property relations between the spouses as well as their inheritance rights and those of their children. Therefore marriage is intrinsically a government concern.

In addition to these time-honored beliefs, the founders brought a more modern idea to the matrimonial drafting table. Like many of their educated contemporaries in Western Europe, they had come to think of marriage in a way congruent with emerging ideals of individual liberty and democratic equality. In the Old World, marriage was originally a matter of caste, class, or clan. Courtship was closer in spirit to bartering than romance; young people of means were to be traded off by elders intent on solidifying family ties and merging family fortunes and acres.

By the late eighteenth century, however, Western Europeans were increasingly emphasizing marriage as a love-match between two self-determining individuals. Young people were free to choose for themselves with whom to spend their lives, and love might transcend class barriers to recognize the intrinsic personal worth of the beloved. This is the lesson of the profoundly democratic novels of Samuel Richardson and Charlotte Brontë, in which the drama concerns a rich, wellborn master coming to realize that he loves his servant, that she is a character of sterling worth, and that he should marry rather than merely seduce her. In the same vein, the novels of Jane Austen dramatize what she understood was turning into one of life's most momentous, morally fraught decisions. For if the young could freely choose their own spouses, they needed to do so wisely, transcending mere sexual attraction and judging their suitors' worth in the moral rather than the economic sense. Even so, at the time of the founding of the American republic, these modern ideas were still more theory than practice in Europe, where arranged marriages remained the norm among the elite.

The founders wanted to clear away many of the traditions that had kept these democratic notions from taking firm hold in old Europe. American marriage would reflect American principles of liberty and self-government. Unlike the hordes of serfs, servants, and subjects in other parts of the world, American citizens would shape their own lives and determine their country's destiny. Just as citizens would be self-governing in the political realm, they would also choose their spouses freely. According to Nancy F. Cott's *Public Vows: A History of Marriage and the Nation* (the source for much of the history of marriage in America that follows), since the struggle against domination and coercion was the essence of the American nation, the young needed to be free from arranged marriages and the authoritarian fathers who contracted them. As the historian Jay Fliegelman has observed, the American Revolution and the new Western seriousness about romantic love, which developed at the same time, both sprang from a heightened valuation of the ideal of self-determination.

Essential as it was, the loving, self-chosen vow was only one ingredient in the recipe for self-government. Self-government also meant citizenly self-reliance. The founders believed that American citizens should not only be allowed to run their own lives but should be capable of and responsible for doing so. In order to be free from "authority in all its guises," as Jefferson put it, citizens had to be competent, industrious, self-sufficient, and virtuous. All these qualities were to be learned in the republican home: "The foundations of national morality must be laid in private families," John Adams wrote in his diary in 1778.

Here Adams was voicing an up-to-the-minute theory of the republican family. Political thinkers imagined the American family as a factory specifically designed to turn out self-governing citizens—something quite different from what other kinds of families did. They believed that the affectionate ties between spouses led to civic responsibility: marriage based on individual choice would promote trust and equality that could then be projected into public life. "In detaching us from self, [love] accustoms us to attach ourselves the more to others. . . . [T]he lover becomes a husband, a parent, a citizen," a 1791 essay in *New-York Magazine* put it. In addition, the founders recognized, the colonists' pioneer past had already made the American family an unusually and dependably self-reliant and industrious unit, just as later, when the nation expanded westward, the frontier family became a byword for rugged and indomitable self-sufficiency.

Most important, republican marriage provided the edifice in which couples would care for and socialize their children to meet the demands of the new political order. If republican marriage celebrated self-government, it also had to pass its principles to the young; it was supposed to perpetuate as well as embody the habits of freedom. So whereas in all Western societies the state concerns itself with fostering the institution of the family because it is the mechanism by which the society reproduces itself, in America that state concern takes on a special urgency because of child-rearing's unique momentousness to the national project.

The small size of American families helped here. As any soccer mom or dad knows, parents with two or three children can invest far more attention in each individual child than those with eight or ten. By the Jacksonian period, the size of American families began to shrink. According to Janet Brodie's *Contraception and Abortion in Nineteenth-Century America*, the number of children born to white native-born women declined by 49 percent in the nineteenth century, from an average of seven children in 1800 to 3.6 by 1900.

Demographers usually explain the drop in fertility as the result of improvements in infant mortality rates and a shift away from a strictly agrarian economy, in which large families were an advantage. But it's also likely that republican parents were discovering that preparing children for self-government was a mammoth undertaking, more demanding than socializing children to thrive in more communal societies.

Early republican child-rearing experts emphasized to American parents that they were responsible for creating independent, industrious, and resourceful future citizens. American children should be brought up to be active, observant thinkers. "All the faculties of a child's mind should be cultivated," wrote Lydia Child in *Mother's Book*; kids should develop "habits of attention and activity of mind."

American theorists also encouraged parents to abandon the demand for absolute, fearful obedience that was a relic of the Old World. Children preparing for life in the new country could not remain mere passive subjects within an Old World patriarchal family. Whippings and beatings, commonplace throughout much of the world, were to be used only as a last resort; punishment "should be threatened as seldom as possible, and next as seldom executed as possible," the clergyman and child expert Horace Bushnell wrote in 1849. This kinder, gentler discipline was designed to get children to behave virtuously because they had internalized national values, not because they feared either external authority or the shame they would bring on their families.

To hear foreign travelers of the early nineteenth century tell it, the republican couple maintaining the homestead or going to church with its republican offspring was noticeably different—though admittedly, there was a downside.

British naval officer and author Captain Frederick Marryat wrote of a scene that he witnessed during a visit to the United States in 1839. He watched a three-year-old named Johnny, whose mother had called him to come in out of the cold. "I won't!" the boy answered. "Come, my sweet, I've something for you," his mother implored. "I won't," Johnny pouted. His father took the more patriarchal approach and ordered his son inside. "I won't," the child insisted yet again. "A sturdy republican!" the father exclaimed, smiling, to the captain, who, being from the old world, was standing aghast.

The founders probably didn't foresee republican children quite like Johnny, but such "sturdiness" may have been inevitable in families in which the young had some freedom to question authority. Marryat may have been disdainful, but other European observers of the new world, including Alexis de Tocqueville, were impressed by the egalitarian, youthful spirit of the American family, which they contrasted with their own stuffy, patriarchal households. Unlike "the respectful and frigid observances of aristocratic families," Tocqueville observed, democratic families enjoy a "familiar intimacy, which renders authority less absolute. . . . [A] species of equality prevails around the domestic hearth." The new political order was placing unprecedented emphasis on individual rights, personal choice, and equality; the new domestic order appeared to be doing the same.

You won't hear much about this historical background in the current debate over marriage, but advocates for gay marriage certainly invoke fragments of the American past in their argument. They frequently compare the current predicament of gays with that of other minorities, particularly African Americans, in the days before they had full rights to marriage. History, they argue, shows us that marriage is a civil right that has expanded over time to include previously marginalized groups; gays now deserve those rights as well. "Throughout the history of Massachusetts, marriage has been in a state of change," a group of historians of marriage, family, and the law asserted in an *amicus* brief in the case that legalized gay marriage in the state. Gay marriage "represents the logical next step in this court's long tradition of reforming marriage to fit the evolving nature of committed intimate relationships and the rights of the individuals in those relationships." But detaching the "tradition of reforming marriage" from the multifaceted tradition of republican marriage not only starts history around 1968, it also presents a seriously distorted picture of why the American government is in the marriage business at all.

While gays often invoke the black/homosexual analogy to assert in a general way that anti-homosexual sentiments are as vicious and irrational as racism, gay-marriage advocates use the comparison much more specifically. Their most commonly repeated argument goes like this: denying homosexuals the right to marry whom they wish is little different from denying blacks the right to marry whites, an injustice written into many state law books well into the twentieth century. It was not until 1967 that the Supreme Court, in *Loving v. Virginia*, finally ruled that state bans on such intermarriage were a violation of the Fourteenth Amendment's equal-protection clause. "Marriage is one of the basic civil rights of man," Chief Justice Earl Warren wrote in his decision, in words that have become a familiar refrain in the current debate. The court rested its decision on one important pillar in the sophisticated architecture of republican marriage: that marriage is a civil contract. If the Fourteenth Amendment protects the right of black citizens to enter into a mortgage agreement or take out a car loan, it certainly protects their right to marry whomever they choose. It is logically inescapable, gay-marriage advocates conclude, that the same goes for homosexuals.

And it would be logical—if a pillar were the same thing as the whole building. That the state has an interest in upholding the civil rights of individuals who want to marry doesn't mean that's the only interest it has in the institution. The state also has a strong—even a life-and-death—interest in marriage as the environment in which the next generation of its citizens is raised.

An earlier chapter in the history of African-American marriage illustrates this point. After the Civil War, anti-slavery Republicans were alarmed by the promiscuity and rampant fatherlessness among ex-slaves, disastrous consequences of the institution's prohibition against slaves entering into marriage contracts. These abolitionists created the Freedmen's Bureau, in part as a federal marriage initiative: they wanted to encourage ex-slaves to marry and create stable families. Their aim wasn't primarily to ensure the civil right of blacks to enter into contracts of all sorts, including marriage; they believed, above all, that American-style marriage would help ex-slaves become responsible, self-reliant citizens who would rear responsible, self-reliant children. In light of this dual state concern—the rights of the couple *and* the promotion of self-governing families that would mirror and sustain the republic—the historical analogy between black marriage and gay marriage that the advocates posit makes no sense.

In fact, gay-marriage proponents generally treat children as a distraction from the state's interest in marriage rather than crucial to it. They impatiently insist that history has settled the matter: it has definitively separated child-rearing and marriage, demonstrating conclusively that marriage is a changing and elastic institution that can easily accommodate homosexuals. "When a third of children are born out of wedlock, when contraception and abortion are available on demand, when you have single-parent adoption legal in every state," Jonathan Rauch, the author of the recent *Gay Marriage*, has written, "the debate is over about detaching marriage from parenthood—indeed was over years ago." Andrew Sullivan, along with Rauch one of the most thoughtful and eloquent advocates writing today, agrees: the argument that marriage has anything to do with children, he says, "fails socially and culturally because in our culture at this time, procreation is not understood to be an essential part of what it is to be married."

But it's worth considering just how recently—and how haphazardly—Americans closed "the debate . . . about detaching marriage from parenthood." For most of American history, republican marriage remained the reigning paradigm: a self-reliant and child-centered couple, who had freely chosen each other in a spirit of equality and mutual affection and who would pass on to their young not just property but also the qualities needed to live in freedom. That reign came to an end only in the late 1960s as divorce laws loosened and Americans began pulling off their wedding rings at record rates.

Divorce is such a conundrum for the nation because it follows directly from American principles even while threatening to subvert them. During the Revolutionary Era, marriage theorists understood that a nation that loves liberty had to tolerate some divorce; if it was a matter of principle that you chose to enter into wedlock, it was also a matter of principle that you had to have some way of choosing to get out, at least under some circumstances. A number of early writers—including Thomas Paine, whose problems with Mrs. Paine gave him a personal stake in the issue—urged Americans to take a tolerant approach toward the practice. Still, even though divorce was more accepted in this country than in many parts of the world, it remained rare, a last resort and one that worried people deeply. That was no longer the case by the late 1960s, when squeamishness on the subject evaporated, the marital exit door flew open, and not only the battered and the miserable but also the merely unfulfilled came pouring out.

This shift was a threat to republican marriage for reasons that went beyond a mushrooming population of newly single mothers scraping together funds to pay their rent or their baby-sitters while their children trekked across the country to visit dad every school vacation. The soaring rates of divorce signaled a fundamental transformation in the American idea of marriage. As Americans crowded into the divorce courts, they were casting aside the complex—and demanding—vision of the founders. Marriage was becoming a minimalist institution; people now thought of it as an intimate relationship between two adults, having little to do with children and nothing to do with propagating the political and moral culture.

This demand for a fuller recognition of the individual rights of spouses who sought divorce, along with the loosening relationship between child-rearing and marriage—both necessary precursors for gay marriage—led inexorably to a further development. If marriage was simply a personal relationship between adults and had little to do with child-rearing, Americans wondered, what was the problem with a woman's having a baby if she wasn't wearing a ring? The answer could only be that there was none.

What did the law have to say about this cultural revolution, given the state's interest in protecting marriage as the institution in which children are raised? The courts, in all their wisdom, decided that safeguarding marriage wasn't their job any more. In case after case, judges decreed that marriage was an ordinary civil contract and that marriage and child-rearing were legally unconnected. Never mind that American law and policy had always accepted the traditional assumption that marriage laws centered largely on the relationship between generations. That was history. In the 1972 *Stanley v. Illinois* case, to cite just one of many examples, the Supreme Court decided that custody laws distinguishing wed and unwed fathers were "constitutionally repugnant." Fathers who had never married their child's mother should have the same rights as those who had. More recently the prestigious American Law Institute recommended that state family law be updated to treat cohabiting parents as virtually identical to married parents in the event of a breakup. Sometimes parents marry; sometimes they don't. Why should the state care?

Many have interpreted these legal innovations as part of the "long tradition of reforming marriage" in America that includes giving wives more rights over their own property as well as the repeal of miscegenation laws. They were no such thing. Unlike the changes in the treatment of blacks and women, which more fully expressed the founders' ideals, the divorce revolution and the consequent change in thinking about marriage and child-rearing represented a hard turn away from the original republican model.

Widespread divorce and illegitimacy fracture into pieces the founders' ideals of the self-governing family. Republican marriage had been a great experiment to harness a universal family bond into the service of a particular view of human freedom. Every society has some kind of marriage to tie parents and their offspring together, but only the American form of marriage strove to allow individuals the greatest amount of freedom within that tie. Little did the founders expect that their most treasured ideal, freedom, would eventually be turned against the institution they most prized for promoting that liberty by nurturing free citizens.

No one knows the personal destruction wrought during this history better than the children who were its victims. For the generation now in its twenties and thirties, the sundering of child-rearing and marriage was not part of the musty past; it was a bitter and lived reality. The world they grew up in was a scary, unpredictable place of self-absorbed adults who had a habit of disappearing, only to pop up from time to time with a stranger introduced as a new member of the family.

That's not the world they want for their own children. Few of them are familiar with founding thinkers like James Wilson or John Adams, but they know enough to see that the family life the founders had in mind was better than the one they endured. Yankelovich Partners found in one poll that almost three-quarters of Gen Xers—that is, adults in their late twenties and thirties—said they'd favor a return to more traditional standards in family life, though only a little more than half of their boomer parents agree. Knowing firsthand what it feels like when your father sits you down at the kitchen table and, unable to look you in the eye, says, "Your mother and I don't love each other any more"—and knowing from personal experience that their own capacity for stable relationships is shaky as a result—this generation questions a regime of drive-through divorces. A 1994 study by the National Opinion Research Center found that Gen Xers were the age group least likely to say that divorce is the best option for troubled couples. Young parents in their twenties and thirties are "nostalgic for the childhood that boomers supposedly had," as *American Demographics* has put it. "It's informed their model of the perfect, traditional marriage."

So what are we to make of the fact that these mom-and-apple-pie young people tend to be more in favor of gay marriage than their parents and grandparents are? The great irony is that their traditionalism enlarges their sympathy for gays' hunger for 'til-death-do-us-part commitment; after all, that's what they want too. Odd as it sounds, gays and the children who grew up in single-parent homes share the experience of standing outside and looking longingly through the window at the peaceful, Norman Rockwell family reading or playing Scrabble in front of the fireplace. Rauch and Sullivan, in particular, have written touchingly of marriage as a solemn, even spiritual, union, a momentous public vow to another person that comes with profound responsibilities and aspires to transcendence. If you add together young people's earnest devotion to marriage and their interest in the civil rights movement (insofar as they have studied any American history at all, it's likely to begin with Rosa Parks and end with Martin Luther King), you have a generation for which gay marriage seems merely commonsensical.

But what the young neo-traditionalists have trouble understanding is that their embrace of the next civil rights revolution, as many of them are inclined to see the fight for gay marriage, is actually at war with their longing for a more stable domestic life. Gay marriage gives an enfeebled institution another injection of the toxin that got it sick in the first place: it reinforces the definition of marriage as a loving, self-determining couple engaging in an ordinary civil contract that has nothing to do with children. That's no way for marriage to get its gravitas back. It is marriage's dedication to child-rearing, to a future that projects far beyond the passing feelings of a couple, that has the potential to discipline adult passion. "The gravity of marriage as an institution comes from its demand that love be negotiated through these larger responsibilities [surrounding procreation]," Shelby Steele has written in response to Andrew Sullivan. Ignore those responsibilities and you get, well, you get the marital meltdown that this generation was hoping to transform.

There is another reason to be skeptical about the idea that gay marriage is another step forward in an unbroken history of social progress. In fact, as we saw in the preceding chapter, the fraying of the bond between marriage and child-rearing over the past decades has been a step backward: it has increased poverty and inequality. Single-parent families, whether divorced or never married, are often poor—and very much poorer than their two-earner counterparts. Instead of being the self-reliant units the founders envisioned, too many of them depend on a powerful nanny state, either for welfare payments or for determining custody and tracking down child support. And instead of being the self-governing institutions of republican theory—nurturing sturdy, self-governing citizens—single-parent families, as many studies have shown, bring up kids who as adults do markedly poorer on average in school, career, and marriage than those who grew up in intact two-parent families. As for children of never-married mothers: many of them make up the permanent underclass, and their high rates of crime, school failure, and welfare dependency are everything the founders expected the republican family to prevent. That so many of these families are black would make the Reconstruction architects of the Freedmen's Bureau weep.

Think of the past several decades of high rates of divorce and illegitimacy as a kind of natural experiment testing the truth of the founders' vision. The results are in: if we forget that marriage is both a voluntary union between two loving partners and an arrangement for rearing the next generation of self-reliant citizens, our capacity for self-government weakens.

Alongside the familiar anthropological truth that marriage comes in many forms is another truth you don't hear about so much: different kinds of marriage—not to mention nonmarriage—mold different kinds of individuals. The founders envisioned a very specific sort of institution, one that would nourish a republic of equal, self-governing citizens. The evolution of marriage over the past forty years has undermined that vision. Gay marriage threatens to weaken it even further.

The next four essays amount to a case study of what happens when marriage disappears, for that is what has happened in the black community. Daniel Patrick Moynihan warned of this impending disaster in 1965, but the nation, on the verge of a cultural revolution that insisted things be otherwise, was in no mood to listen. Instead elites built an elaborate edifice of denial and rationalization whose ruins spoil the political landscape to this day and whose consequences continue to roil the inner city.

Moynihan warned that when boys grew up without fathers, they would run wild. Women, he cautioned, would be unable to control their sons and incapable of modeling the ways of honorable manhood. But even Moynihan understated the problems of a marriageless culture. When marriage disappeared from the inner city, so did many of the bourgeois norms and routines it embodied. An especially crucial loss was the middle-class life script, the planned sequence of life events that taught young people the best route into a successful life. In almost every culture, marriage has marked the onset of adulthood, the moment when society anoints a young individual as fully responsible to care for the next generation. Without marriage, black young people have stumbled into adulthood without a blueprint. Children, as it was often said, began having children. Fathers vanished. Men lost the signpost directing them toward a meaningful future. And parents, immature and isolated from the middle-class vision symbolized by marriage, failed to provide their children a way out.

From their perch in academia and in foundations, experts, assuming that middle-class norms were the default position, did not understand what was happening. To explain the increasing chaos of the black family and of inner-city neighborhoods, they looked to what they called "structural factors," by which they mostly meant the disappearance of manufacturing jobs. What the experts failed to grasp was that with marriage gone, blacks had lost an institution that contained a good deal of inherited wisdom about how to live full, successful lives.

3

The Black Family: Forty-plus Years of Lies

Read through the megazillion words on class, income mobility, and poverty in the 2005 *New York Times* series "Class Matters" and you still won't grasp two of the most basic truths on the subject: (1) entrenched, multigenerational poverty is largely black, and (2) it is intricately intertwined with the collapse of the nuclear family in the inner city. The truth is that we are now a two-family nation, separate and unequal—one thriving and intact, the other struggling, broken, and far too often African-American.

So why does the *Times*, like so many who rail against inequality, fall silent on the relation between poverty and single-parent families? To answer that question—and to continue the confrontation with facts that Americans still prefer not to mention in polite company—you have to go back to 1965. That was when a resounding cry of outrage echoed throughout Washington and the civil rights movement in reaction to Daniel Patrick Moynihan's Department of Labor report warning that the ghetto family was in disarray. Entitled

"The Negro Family: The Case for National Action," the prophetic report prompted civil rights leaders, academics, politicians, and pundits to make a momentous—and, as time has shown, tragically wrong—decision about how to frame the national discussion about poverty.

To go back to the political and social moment before the battle over the Moynihan Report broke out is to return to a time before the country's discussion of black poverty had hardened into fixed orthodoxies—before phrases like "blaming the victim," "self-esteem," "out-of-wedlock child-bearing" (the term at the time was "illegitimacy"), and even "teen pregnancy" had become current. While solving the black poverty problem seemed an immense political challenge, as a conceptual matter it didn't seem like rocket science. Most analysts assumed that once the nation removed discriminatory legal barriers and expanded employment opportunities, blacks would advance, just as poor immigrants had.

Conditions for testing that proposition looked good. Between the 1954 *Brown* school desegregation decision and the Civil Rights Act of 1964, legal racism had been dismantled. And the economy was humming along; in the first five years of the sixties it generated seven million jobs.

Yet those most familiar with what was called "the Negro problem" were growing nervous. About half of all blacks had moved into the middle class by the mid-sixties, but now progress seemed to be stalling. The rise in black income relative to that of whites, steady throughout the fifties, was sputtering to a halt. More blacks were out of work in 1964 than in 1954. Most alarming, after rioting in Harlem and Paterson, New Jersey, in 1964, the problems of the Northern ghettos suddenly seemed more intractable than those of the George Wallace South.

Moynihan, then assistant secretary of labor and one of a new class of government social scientists, was among the worriers as he puzzled over his charts. One in particular caught his eye. Instead of rates of black male unemployment and welfare enrollment running parallel as they always had, in 1962 they began to diverge in a way that would come to be called "Moynihan's scissors." In the past, policymakers had assumed that if the male heads of household had jobs, women and children would be provided for. This no longer seemed true. Even while more black men—though still "catastrophically" low numbers—were getting jobs, more black women were joining the welfare rolls. Moynihan and his aides decided that a serious analysis was in order.

Convinced that "the Negro revolution . . . , a movement for equality as well as for liberty," was now at risk, Moynihan wanted to make several arguments in his report. The first was empirical and would quickly become indisputable: single-parent families were on the rise in the ghetto. But other points were more speculative and sparked a partisan dispute that has lasted to this day. Moynihan argued that the rise in single-mother families was not due to a lack of jobs but rather to a destructive vein in ghetto culture that could be traced back to slavery and Jim Crow discrimination. Although the black sociologist E. Franklin Frazier had already introduced the idea in the 1930s, Moynihan's argument defied conventional social-science wisdom. As he wrote later, "The work began in the most orthodox setting, the U.S. Department of Labor, to establish at some level of statistical conciseness what 'everyone knew': that economic conditions determine social conditions. Whereupon, it turned out that what everyone knew was evidently not so."

But Moynihan went much further than merely overthrowing familiar explanations about the cause of poverty. He also described, through pages of disquieting charts and graphs, the emergence of a "tangle of pathology," including delinquency, joblessness, school failure, crime, and fatherlessness that characterized ghetto—or what would come to be called underclass—behavior. Moynihan may have borrowed the term "pathology" from Kenneth Clark's *The Dark Ghetto*, also published that year. But as both a descendant and a scholar of what he called "the wild Irish slums"—he had written a chapter on the poor Irish in the classic *Beyond the Melting Pot*—the assistant secretary of labor was no stranger to ghetto self-destruction. He knew the dangers it posed to "the basic socializing unit" of the family. And he suspected that the risks were magnified in the case of blacks since their "matriarchal" family had the effect of underemploying men, leaving them adrift and "alienated."

More than most social scientists, Moynihan, steeped in history and anthropology, understood what families do. They "shape their children's character and ability," he wrote. "By and large, adult conduct in society is learned as a child." What children learned in the "disorganized home[s]" of the ghetto, as he described through his forest of graphs, was that adults do not finish school, get jobs, or, in the case of men, take care of their children or obey the law. Marriage, on the other hand, provides a "stable home" for children to learn common virtues. Implicit in Moynihan's analysis was that marriage orients men and women toward the future, asking them not just to commit to each other but to plan, to earn, to save, and to devote themselves to advancing their children's prospects. Single mothers in the ghetto, on the other hand, tended to drift into pregnancy, often more than once and by more than one man, and to float through the chaos around them. Such mothers are unlikely to "shape their children's character and ability" in ways that lead to upward mobility. Separate and unequal families, in other words, meant that blacks would have their liberty but would be strangers to equality. Hence Moynihan's conclusion: "a national effort towards the problems of Negro Americans must be directed towards the question of family structure."

Astonishingly, even for that surprising time, the Johnson administration agreed. Prompted by Moynihan's still-unpublished study, Johnson delivered a speech at the Howard University commencement that called for "the next and more profound stage of the battle for civil rights." The president began his speech with the era's conventional civil rights language, condemning inequality and calling for more funding of medical care, training, and education for Negroes. But he also broke into new territory, analyzing the family problem with what strikes the contemporary ear as shocking candor. He announced: "Negro poverty is not white poverty." He described "the breakdown of the Negro family structure," which he said was "the consequence of ancient brutality, past injustice and present prejudice." "When the family collapses, it is the children that are usually damaged," Johnson continued. "When it happens on a massive scale, the community itself is crippled."

Johnson was to call this his "greatest civil rights speech," but he was just about the only one to see it that way. By late summer the Moynihan Report that was the speech's inspiration was under attack from all sides. Civil servants in the "permanent government" at Health, Education, and Welfare (HEW) and at the Children's Bureau muttered about the report's "subtle racism." Academics picked apart its statistics. Black leaders like Congress of Racial Equality (CORE) director Floyd McKissick scolded that, rather than the family, "It's the damn system that needs changing."

In part the hostility was an accident of timing. Just days after the Moynihan Report was leaked to *Newsweek* in early August, L.A.'s Watts ghetto exploded. Televised images of South Central Los Angeles rioters burning down their own neighborhood collided in the public mind with the contents of the report. Some concluded that the "tangle of pathology" was the administration's explanation for urban riots, a view quite at odds with civil rights leaders' determination to portray the violence as an outpouring of black despair over white injustice. Moreover, given the fresh wounds of segregation, the persistent brutality against blacks, and the ugly tenaciousness of racism, the fear of white backsliding and the sense of injured pride that one can hear in so many of Moynihan's critics are entirely understandable.

Less forgivable was the refusal to grapple seriously— either at the time or in the months, years, even decades to come—with the basic cultural insight contained in the report: that ghetto families were at risk of raising generations of children unable to seize the opportunity that the civil rights movement had opened up for them. Instead, critics changed the subject, accusing Moynihan—wrongfully, as any honest reading of "The Negro Family" proves—of ignoring joblessness and discrimination. Family instability is a "peripheral issue," warned Whitney Young, executive director of the National Urban League. "The problem is discrimination." The protest generating the most buzz came from William Ryan, a CORE activist, in "Savage Discovery: The Moynihan Report," published in *The Nation* and later reprinted in the NAACP's official publication. Ryan, though a psychologist, did not hear Moynihan's point that as the family goes, so go the children. He heard code for the archaic charge of black licentiousness. He described the report as a "highly sophomoric treatment of illegitimacy" and insisted that whites' broader access to abortion, contraception, and adoption hid the fact that they were no less "promiscuous" than blacks. Most memorably, he accused Moynihan of "blaming the victim," a phrase that would become the title of his 1971 book and the fear-inducing censor of future plainspeaking about the ghetto's decay.

That Ryan's phrase turned out to have more cultural staying power than anything in the Moynihan Report is a tragic emblem of the course of the subsequent discussion about the ghetto family. For white liberals and the black establishment, poverty became a zero-sum game: either you believed, as they did, that there was a defect in the system, or you believed that there was a defect in the individual. It was as if critiquing the family meant that you supported inferior schools, even that you were a racist. Although "The Negro Family" had been a masterpiece of complex analysis which implied that individuals were intricate parts of a variety of systems—familial, cultural, and economic—it gave birth to a hardened either/or politics from which the country has barely recovered.

By autumn, when a White House conference on civil rights took place, the Moynihan Report, initially planned as its centerpiece, had disappeared. Johnson himself, having just introduced large numbers of ground troops into Vietnam, went mum on the subject, steering clear of the word "family" in his next State of the Union message. This was a moment when the nation had the resources, the leadership (the president had been overwhelmingly elected, and he had the largest majorities in the House and Senate since the New Deal), and the will "to make a total . . . commitment to the cause of Negro equality," Moynihan lamented in a 1967 postmortem of his report in *Commentary*. Instead, he declared, the nation had disastrously decided to punt on Johnson's "next and more profound stage in the battle for civil rights." "The issue of the Negro family was dead."

Well, not exactly. Over the next fifteen years the black family question actually became a growth industry inside academe, the foundations, and the government. But it wasn't the same family that had worried Moynihan and that in the real world continued to self-destruct at unprecedented rates. Scholars invented a fantasy family—strong and healthy, a poor man's Brady Bunch—whose function was not to reflect truth but to soothe injured black self-esteem and bolster the emerging feminist critique of male privilege, bourgeois individualism, and the nuclear family. The literature of this period was so evasive, so implausible, so far removed from what was really unfolding in the ghetto that if you didn't know better, you might conclude that people actually *wanted* to keep the black family separate and unequal.

Consider one of the first books out of the gate, *Black Families in White America*, by Andrew Billingsley, published in 1968 and still referred to as "seminal." "Unlike Moynihan and others, we do not view the Negro as a causal nexus in a 'tangle of pathologies' which feeds on itself," he declared. "[The Negro family] is, in our view, an absorbing, adaptive, and amazingly resilient mechanism for the socialization of its children and the civilization of its society." Pay no attention to the 25 percent of poor ghetto families, Billingsley urged. Think instead about the 75 percent of black middle-class families—though Moynihan had made a special point of exempting them from his report.

Other black-pride–inspired scholars looked at female-headed families and declared them authentically African and therefore a *good* thing. In a related vein, Carol Stack published *All Our Kin*, a 1974 HEW-funded study of families in a Midwestern ghetto with many multigenerational female households. In an implicit criticism of American individualism, Stack depicted "The Flats," as she dubbed her setting, as a vibrant and cooperative urban village, where mutual aid—including from sons, brothers, and uncles, who provided financial support and strong role models for children—created "a tenacious, active, lifelong network."

In fact, some scholars continued, maybe the nuclear family was really just a toxic white hang-up anyway. No one asked what nuclear families did, or how they prepared children for a modern economy. The important point was simply that they were not black. "One must question the validity of the white middle-class lifestyle from its very foundation because it has already proven itself to be decadent and unworthy of emulation," wrote Joyce Ladner (who later became the first female president of Howard University) in her 1972 book *Tomorrow's Tomorrow*. Robert Hill of the Urban League, who published *The Strengths of Black Families* that same year, claimed to have uncovered science that proved Ladner's point: "Research studies have revealed that many one-parent families are more intact or cohesive than many two-parent families: data on child abuse, battered wives and runaway children indicate higher rates among two-parent families in suburban areas than one-parent families in inner-city communities." That science, needless to say, was as reliable as a deadbeat dad.

Feminists, similarly fixated on overturning the "oppressive ideal of the nuclear family," also welcomed this dubious scholarship. Convinced that marriage was the main arena of male privilege, feminists projected onto the struggling single mother an image of the "strong black woman" who had always had to work and who was "superior in terms of [her] ability to function healthily in the world," as Toni Morrison put it. The lucky black single mother could also enjoy more equal relationships with men than her miserably married white sisters.

If black pride made it hard to grapple with the increasingly separate and unequal family, feminism made it impossible. Fretting about single-parent families was now not only racist but also sexist, an effort to deny women their independence, their sexuality, or both. As for the poverty of single mothers, that was simply more proof of patriarchal oppression. In 1978, University of Wisconsin researcher Diana Pearce introduced the useful term "feminization of poverty." But for her and her many allies, the problem was not the crumbling of the nuclear family; it was the lack of government support for single women and the failure of business to pay women their due.

With the benefit of embarrassed hindsight, academics today sometimes try to wave away these notions as the justifiably angry but ultimately harmless speculations of political and academic activists. "The depth and influence of the radicalism of the late 1960s and early 1970s are often exaggerated," historian Stephanie Coontz writes in her book *Marriage, a History: From Obedience to Intimacy, or How Love Conquered Marriage*. This is pure revisionism. The radical delegitimation of the family was so pervasive that even people at the center of power joined in. It made no difference that so many of these cheerleaders for single mothers had themselves spent their lives in traditional families and probably would rather have cut off an arm than seen their own unmarried daughters pushing strollers.

Take, for instance, Supreme Court Justice William Brennan, who wrote a concurring assent in the 1977 *Moore v. City of East Cleveland* decision. The case concerned a woman and her grandson evicted from a housing project following a city ordinance that defined "family" as parents—or parent—and their own children. Brennan did not simply agree that the Court should rule in favor of the grandmother—a perfectly reasonable position. He also assured the Court that "the extended family has many strengths not shared by the nuclear family." Relying on Robert Hill's "science," he declared that delinquency, addiction, crime, "neurotic disabilities," and mental illness were more prevalent in societies where "autonomous nuclear families prevail," a conclusion that would have bewildered the writers of the Constitution that Brennan was supposedly interpreting.

In its bumbling way and with far-reaching political consequences, the executive branch also offered warm greetings to the single-parent family. Alert to growing apprehension about the state of the American family during his 1976 presidential campaign, Jimmy Carter had promised a conference on the subject. Clearly less concerned with conditions in the ghetto than with satisfying feminist advocates, the administration named a black single (divorced) mother to lead the event, occasioning an outcry from conservatives. By 1980, when it finally convened after numerous postponements, the White House Conference on the Family had morphed into the White House Conference on Families, to signal that all family forms were equal.

Instead of the political victory for moderate Democrats that Carter had expected, the conference galvanized religious conservatives. Later, conservative heavyweight Paul Weyrich observed that the Carter conference marked the moment when religious activists moved in force into Republican politics. Doubtless they were also more energized by their own issues of feminism and gay rights than by what was happening in the ghetto. But their new rallying cry of "family values" nonetheless became a political dividing line, with unhappy fallout for liberals for years to come.

Meanwhile the partisans of single motherhood got a perfect chance to test their theories, since the urban ghettos were fast turning into nuclear-family-free zones. Indeed, by 1980, fifteen years after "The Negro Family," the out-of-wedlock birthrate among blacks had more than doubled, to 56 percent. In the ghetto that number was considerably higher, as high as 66 percent in New York City. Many experts comforted themselves by pointing out that white mothers were also beginning to forgo marriage, but the truth was that only 9 percent of white births occurred out of wedlock.

And how was the black single-parent family doing? It would be fair to say that it had not been exhibiting the strengths of kinship networks. According to numbers crunched by Moynihan and economist Paul Offner, of the black children born between 1967 and 1969, 72 percent received Aid to Families with Dependent Children before the age of eighteen. School dropout rates, delinquency, and crime, among the other dysfunctions that Moynihan had warned about, were rising in the cities. In short, the fifteen years since the report was written had witnessed both the birth of millions of fatherless babies and the entrenchment of an underclass.

Liberal advocates had two main ways of dodging the subject of family collapse while still addressing its increasingly alarming fallout. The first, largely the creation of Marian Wright Edelman, who in 1973 founded the Children's Defense Fund, was to talk about children not as the offspring of individual mothers and fathers responsible for rearing them, but as an oppressed class living in generic, nebulous, and never-to-be-analyzed "families." Framing the problem of ghetto children in this way, CDF was able to mount a powerful case for a host of services, from prenatal care to day care to housing subsidies, in the name of children's developmental needs, which did not seem to include either a stable domestic life or, for that matter, fathers. Advocates like Edelman might not have viewed the collapsing ghetto family as a welcome occurrence, but they treated it as a kind of natural event, like drought, beyond human control and judgment. As recently as 2004, marking the fortieth anniversary of the Civil Rights Act, CDF announced on its website: "In 2004 it is morally and economically indefensible that a black preschool child is three times as likely to depend solely on a mother's earnings." This may strike many as a pretty good argument for addressing the prevalence of black single-mother families, but in CDF-speak it is a case for federal natural-disaster relief.

The Children's Defense Fund was only the best-known child-advocacy group to impose a gag rule on the role of fatherless families in the plight of its putative constituents. The Carnegie Corporation followed suit. In 1977 it published a highly influential report by Kenneth Keniston called *All Our Children: The American Family Under Pressure*. It makes an obligatory nod toward the family's role in raising children, before calling for a cut in unemployment, a federal job guarantee, national health insurance, affirmative action, and a host of other children's programs. In a review in *Commentary*, Nathan Glazer noted ruefully that *All Our Children* was part of a "recent spate of books and articles on the subject of the family [that] have had little if anything to say about the black family in particular and the matter seems to have been permanently shelved." For that silence, children's advocates deserve much of the credit.

The second way not to talk about what was happening to the ghetto family was to talk instead about teen pregnancy. In 1976 the Alan Guttmacher Institute, Planned Parenthood's research arm, published "Eleven Million Teenagers: What Can Be Done About the Epidemic of Adolescent Pregnancy in the United States?" It was a report that launched a thousand programs. In response to its alarms, HEW chief Joseph Califano helped push through the 1978 Adolescent Health Services and Pregnancy Prevention and Care Act, which funded groups providing services to pregnant adolescents and teen moms. Nonprofits, including the Center for Population Options (now called Advocates for Youth), climbed on the bandwagon. The Ford and Robert Wood Johnson Foundations showered dollars on organizations that ran school-based health clinics; the

Charles Stewart Mott Foundation set up the Too Early Childbearing Network; the Annie E. Casey Foundation sponsored "A Community Strategy for Reaching Sexually Active Adolescents"; and the Carnegie, Ford, and William T. Grant foundations all started demonstration programs.

There was just one small problem: *there was no epidemic of teen pregnancy*. There was an *out-of-wedlock* teen-pregnancy epidemic. Teenagers had gotten pregnant at even higher rates in the past. The numbers had reached their zenith in the 1950s, and the "Eleven Million Teenagers" cited in the Guttmacher Report actually represented a decline in the rate of pregnant teens. Back in the day, however, when they found they were pregnant, girls had either gotten married or given their babies up for adoption. Not this generation. They were used to seeing children growing up without fathers, and they felt no shame about arriving at the maternity ward with no rings on their fingers, even at fifteen.

In the middle-class mind, however, no sane girl would want to have a baby at fifteen—not that experts mouthing rhetoric about the oppressive patriarchal family would admit there was anything wrong with that. That middle-class outlook, combined with post-Moynihan mendacity about the growing disconnect between ghetto childbearing and marriage, led the policy elites to frame what was really the broad cultural problem of separate and unequal families as a simple lack-of-reproductive-services problem. Ergo, girls "at risk" must need sex education and contraceptive services.

But the truth was that underclass girls often *wanted* to have babies; they didn't see it as a problem that they were young and unmarried. They did not follow the middle-class life script that read: protracted adolescence, college, first job, marriage—and only then children. They did not share the belief that children needed mature, educated mothers who would make their youngsters' development the center of their lives. Access to birth control couldn't change any of that.

At any rate, failing to define the problem accurately, advocates were in no position to find the solution. Teen pregnancy not only failed to decline, despite all the public attention, the tens of millions of dollars, and the birth-control pills that were thrown its way. *It went up*—peaking in 1990 at 117 pregnancies per 1,000 teenage girls, up from 105 per 1,000 in 1978 when the Guttmacher Report was published. About 80 percent of those young girls who became mothers were single, and the vast majority would be poor.

Throughout the 1980s the inner city—and the black family—continued to unravel. Child poverty stayed close to 20 percent, hitting a high of 22.7 percent in 1993. Welfare dependency continued to rise, soaring from two million families in 1970 to five million by 1995. By 1990, 65 percent of all black children were being born to unmarried women. In ghetto communities like Central Harlem, the number was closer to 80 percent. By this point, no one doubted that most of these children were destined to grow up poor and to pass down the legacy of single parenting to their own children.

The only good news was that the bad news was so unrelentingly bad that the usual bromides and evasions could no longer hold. Something had to shake up what amounted to an ideological paralysis, and that something came from conservatives. Three thinkers in particular—Charles Murray, Lawrence Mead, and Thomas Sowell—though they did not always write directly about the black family, effectively changed the conversation about it. First, they did not flinch from blunt language in describing the wreckage of the inner city, unafraid of the accusations of racism and victim blaming that came their way. Second, they pointed at the welfare policies of the 1960s, not racism or a lack of jobs or the legacy of slavery, as the cause of inner-city dysfunction, and in so doing they made the welfare mother the public symbol of the ghetto's ills. (Murray in particular argued that welfare money provided a disincentive for marriage, and while his theory may have overstated the role of economics, it's worth noting that he was probably the first to grasp that the country was turning into a nation of separate and unequal families.) And third, they believed that the poor would have to change their behavior instead of waiting for Washington to end poverty, as liberals seemed to be saying.

By the early 1980s the media too had woken up to the ruins of the ghetto family and brought about the return of the repressed Moynihan Report. Declaring Moynihan "prophetic," Ken Auletta, in his 1982 *The Underclass*, proclaimed that "one cannot talk about poverty in America, or about the underclass, without talking about the weakening family structure of the poor." Both the *Baltimore Sun* and the *New York Times* ran series on the black family in 1983, followed by a 1985 *Newsweek* article called "Moynihan: I Told You So" and a 1986 CBS documentary, *The Vanishing Black Family*, produced by Bill Moyers, a onetime aide to Lyndon Johnson, who had supported the Moynihan Report. The most symbolic moment occurred when Moynihan himself gave Harvard's prestigious Godkin Lectures in 1985 in commemoration of the twentieth anniversary of "The Negro Family."

Still, for the most part, liberals were having none of it. They piled on Murray's 1984 *Losing Ground*, ignored Mead and Sowell, and excoriated the word "underclass," which they painted as a recycled and pseudoscientific version of the "tangle of pathology." But there were two important exceptions to the long list of deniers. The first was William Julius Wilson. In his 1987 *The Truly Disadvantaged*, Wilson chastised liberals for being "confused and defensive" and failing to engage "the social pathologies of the ghetto." "The average poor black child today appears to be in the midst of a poverty spell which will last for almost two decades," he warned. Liberals have "to propose thoughtful explanations for the rise in inner-city dislocations." Ironically, though, Wilson's own "mismatch theory" for family breakdown— which hypothesized that the movement of low-skill jobs out of the cities had sharply reduced the number of marriageable black men—had the effect of extending liberal defensiveness about the damaged ghetto family. After all, poor single mothers were only adapting to economic conditions. How could they do otherwise?

The research of another social scientist, Sara McLanahan, was not so easily rationalized, however. A divorced mother herself, McLanahan found Auletta's depiction of her single-parent counterparts in the inner city disturbing, especially because, like other sociologists of the time, she had been taught that the Moynihan Report was the work of a racist—or, at least, a seriously deluded man. But when she surveyed the science available on the subject, she realized that the research was so sparse that no one knew for sure how the children of single mothers were faring. Over the next decade, McLanahan analyzed whatever numbers she could find, and discovered—lo and behold—that children in single-parent homes were not doing as well as children from two-parent homes on a wide variety of measures, from income to school performance to teen pregnancy.

Throughout the late eighties and early nineties, McLanahan presented her emerging findings over protests from feminists and the Children's Defense Fund. Finally in 1994 she published, with Gary Sandefur, *Growing Up with a Single Parent*. McLanahan's research shocked social scientists into reexamining the problem they had presumed was not a problem. It was a turning point. One by one, leading family researchers gradually came around, concluding that McLanahan—and perhaps even Moynihan—was right.

In fact, by the early 1990s, when the ghetto was at its nadir, public opinion had clearly turned. No one was more attuned to this shift than Bill Clinton, who made the family a centerpiece of his domestic policy. In his 1994 State of the Union Address, he announced: "We cannot renew our country when, within a decade, more than half of our children will be born into families where there is no marriage." And in 1996, despite howls of indignation, including from members of his own administration (and mystifyingly, from Moynihan himself), he signed a welfare-reform bill that he had twice vetoed—and that included among its goals increasing the number of children living with their two married parents.

So, have we reached the end of the Moynihan Report saga? That would be vastly overstating matters. Remember: *70 percent of black children are still born to unmarried mothers*. After all that ghetto dwellers have been through, why are so many people still unwilling to call this the calamity it is? Both the National Organization for Women (NOW) and the National Association of Social Workers continue to see marriage as a potential source of female oppression. The Children's Defense Fund still won't touch the subject. Hip-hop culture glamorizes ghetto life: "'cause nowadays it's like a badge of honor / to be a baby mama" go the words to the hit "Baby Mama," which young ghetto mothers view as their anthem. Seriously complicating the issue is the push for gay marriage, which dismissed the formula "children growing up with their own married parents" as a form of discrimination. And then there is the American penchant for to-each-his-own libertarianism. In opinion polls a substantial majority of young people say that having a child outside of marriage is okay—though, judging from their behavior, they seem to mean that it's okay not for them but for other people. Middle- and upper-middle-class Americans act as if they know that marriage provides a structure that protects children's development. If only they were willing to admit it to their fellow citizens.

All told, the nation is at a cultural inflection point that portends change. Although they always caution that "marriage is not a panacea," social scientists almost uniformly accept the research that confirms the benefits for children growing up with their own married parents. Welfare reform and tougher child-support regulations have reinforced the message of personal responsibility for one's children. The Bush administration unabashedly uses the word "marriage" in its welfare policies. Raw numbers support the case for optimism: teen pregnancy, which finally started to decline in the mid-nineties in response to a crisper, teen-pregnancy-is-a-bad-idea cultural message, is now at its lowest rate ever.

And finally, in the ghetto itself there is a growing feeling that mother-only families don't work. That's why, as we'll shortly see, people line up to see an aging comedian as he voices some not-very-funny opinions about their own parenting. That's why so many young men vow to be the fathers they never had. That's why there has been an uptick, albeit small, in the number of black children living with their married parents.

If change really is in the air, it's taken more than forty years to get here—decades of inner-city misery for the country to reach a point at which it fully signed on to the lesson of Moynihan's report. Yes, better late than never; but you could forgive lost generations of ghetto men, women, and children if they found it cold comfort.

4

The Missionary Position

In January 2005 almost two thousand people jammed the auditorium at Wayne County Community College in Detroit to hear Bill Cosby yell at them—there's really no other way to put it—for being bad parents. That was after a crowd had already filled a hall in Newark. And another in Springfield, Massachusetts. And another in Milwaukee. And yet another in Atlanta.

Had Cosby not gone into quarantine as the result of sexual-abuse charges that prosecutors eventually decided not to pursue, there's no question that thousands more poor black parents would have come to town-hall meetings, asking the comedian-activist to harangue them too. They would have waited in line to hear Cosby say the same sort of thing he said in front of the NAACP on the fiftieth anniversary of the Supreme Court's *Brown* decision in May 2004 when he started his crusade: "The lower economic people are not holding up their end of the deal. These people are not parenting!" Or the litany he presented in a Paula Zahn interview: "You got to straighten up your house! Straighten up your apartment! Straighten up your child!" Wearing a sweatshirt with the motto "Parent Power!" he doubtless would have blasted the "poverty pimps and victim pimps" who blame their children's plight on racial injustice. "Proper education has to begin at home. . . . We don't need another federal commission to study the problem. . . . What we need now is parents sitting down with children, overseeing homework, sending children off to school in the morning, well fed, rested, and ready to learn."

Now, Bill Cosby is a big star and all, but at sixty-eight, he's not exactly Beyoncé. Why would people hang from the rafters in order to hear an aging sitcom dad accuse them of raising "knuckleheads"? The commentariat, black and white, sure didn't have an answer. BILLIONAIRE BASHES POOR BLACKS, the *New York Times* headlined columnist Barbara Ehrenreich's attack on Cosby's critique. *Newsweek* columnist Ellis Cose admitted there was some truth to Cosby's charges, but objected, "The basic question is whether criticizing such behavior is enough to change it." Hip-hop entrepreneur Russell Simmons harrumphed an answer to Cose's question: "Judgment of the people in this situation is not helpful." In his Paula Zahn interview, Cosby told how former poet laureate Maya Angelou had chided him in similar terms: "You know, Bill, you're a very nice man, but you have a big mouth."

Well, that's the point, isn't it? Cosby was filling auditoriums precisely because he *has* a big mouth, because he *was* being judgmental. His blunt talk seemed a refreshing tonic to the sense that the standard bromides about the inner city's troubles weren't getting blacks very far. More than forty years after the War on Poverty began, about 30 percent of black children are still living in poverty. Those children face an even chance of dropping out of high school and, according to economist Thomas Hertz, a 42 percent chance of staying in the lowest income decile—far greater than the 17 percent of whites born at the bottom who stay there. After endless attempts at school reform and a gazillion dollars' worth of what policymakers call "interventions," just about everyone realizes—without minimizing the awfulness of ghetto schools—that the problem begins at home and begins early. Yet the assumption among black leaders and poverty experts has long been that you can't expect uneducated, highly stressed parents, often themselves poorly reared, to do all that much about it. Cosby is saying they can.

And about that, he is right.

Let's start with a difficult truth behind Cosby's rant: forty-plus years and trillions of government dollars have not given black and white children equal chances. Put aside the question of the public schools for now; the problem begins way before children first go through their shabby doors. Black kids enter school significantly below their white peers in everything from vocabulary to number awareness to self-control. According to a 1998 National Center for Education Statistics survey of kindergarten teachers, black children are much less likely to show persistence in school tasks, to pay close attention in class, or to seem eager to learn new things than are their white counterparts; Hispanic children fall midway between. As a 2002 book from the liberal Economic Policy Institute, *Inequality at the Starting Gate*, puts it, "[D]isadvantaged [disproportionately black] children start kindergarten with significantly lower cognitive skills than their more advantaged counterparts." Dismayingly, the sentence might have come straight from a government commission on poverty, circa 1964—before the War on Poverty had spent a dime.

And what about Head Start, perhaps the best-known War on Poverty campaign, which was supposed "to bring these kids to the starting line equal," as President Johnson put it at the time? Head Start rested on the reasonable assumption that crucial to fighting poverty was to compensate for what was—or, more to the point, was not—happening at home. If poor kids arrived at school less prepared than their more well-to-do counterparts, well, then, give them more of what those other kids were getting: more stories, building blocks, and puzzles, more talk, more edifying adult attention—as well as good nutrition and health care. Although in retrospect the first Head Start program in the heady summer of 1965—designed to last all of eight weeks—was wildly unrealistic, the approach still made sense. Poor kids would get a concentrated injection of middle-class child-rearing in preschool, and they would start school ready to learn, to achieve at the same rate as their better-off peers, and eventually to live as well as they did.

Except it didn't work out that way. As a lingering reminder of the hopes and idealism that surrounded the War on Poverty, Head Start, with its annual budget of $6.8 billion, remains a sentimental favorite of the public and of Congress. But the truth is, from the first time they parsed the data, Head Start researchers found that while children sometimes enjoyed immediate gains in IQ and social competence, these improvements tended to fade by the time kids hit third grade. The failed promise of Head Start might best be captured by a visit I made several years ago to a Head Start program in a housing project on Manhattan's Lower East Side, a cheerful and orderly place that would satisfy anyone's definition of quality child care. As I was leaving, an administrator introduced me to a young woman of twenty-one or so just arriving with her four-year-old. "This is Sonia," he said proudly. "She went here when she was a little girl." Not only had Head Start failed to prevent a poor child from becoming a teen mother, but a Head Start administrator didn't even seem to think it was supposed to. For him—and, one suspects, for many teachers and parents—Head Start had come to be nothing more than a nice neighborhood preschool. It wasn't meant to change lives, and it boasted with institutional pride of what elite private schools and colleges call legacies.

That doesn't mean preschool has never helped impoverished black children—not by any means. One reason so many are convinced that "Head Start works" is that it is often blurred—sometimes with deliberate fudging by advocates—with several other programs that have had heartening results: the Abecedarian Project at the University of North Carolina and the Perry Preschool in Ypsilanti, Michigan. In 1972, in perhaps the most intensive intervention tried in the United States short of adoption, the Abecedarian Project put fifty-seven very high-risk children into a five-year infant and preschool program where highly trained teachers worked on what child developmentalists call "fine-motor, language, and social-emotional skills." When the kids hit age twenty-one, they still showed some gains over a control group: they had better jobs, three times as many of them went to college, and they were half as likely to be teen parents. The graduates of Perry Preschool, a more conventional two-year program, were less likely than the control group to have been placed in special education or to have been arrested, and were more likely to graduate high school, to have higher monthly earnings as adults, and to own homes.

Still, both these programs were extremely small. Between them a grand total of 115 children enjoyed expertly constructed, exquisitely staffed arrangements, unlikely to be replicable on a large scale. Saying that "preschool works" based on these model programs makes as much sense as saying that because NASA successfully launched a mission to Mars, so can JetBlue.

These days, especially given the public's sticker shock after four decades of government programs, the vast community of child developmentalists and anti-poverty advocates—to its credit—has adopted a more sober tone than at any time since the 1960s. As recently as 1988, War on Poverty veteran Lisbeth Schorr, in her book *Within Our Reach*, trumpeted that success was near: "We now know that the education, health, nutrition, and social services and parent support have prevented and ameliorated many of the educational handicaps associated with growing up in poverty," giving us results that are "measurable and dramatic." (Perry Preschool is one of the three early-childhood programs she cites.) You're not going to hear that kind of talk today. "Do You Believe in Magic?" is the half-bitter title of a 2003 article on preschool intervention by Columbia University Teachers College professor Jeanne Brooks-Gunn, one of the titans of early-childhood research. Edward Zigler, a Head Start founder, has urged experts in the field to "become realistic and temper our hopes." For the bitter truth is that even in the best programs money can buy, we're looking at not equality but damage control, not a middle-class future but "risk prevention."

So why have we been able to make so little headway in improving the life chances of poor black children? One

reason towers over all others, and it's the one Cosby was al-
luding to, however crudely, in his town-hall meetings: poor
black parents rear their children very differently from the
way middle-class parents do, and even by the time the kids
are four years old the results are extremely hard to change.
Academics and poverty mavens know this to be the case,
though they try to soften the harshness of its implications.
They point out—correctly—that poor parents say they
want the same things for their kids that everyone does: a
good job, a nice home, and a satisfying family life. They
observe that poor parents don't have the money or the time
or the psychological well-being to do a lot of the quasi-
educational things that middle-class parents do with their
young children, such as going to the circus or buying Le-
gos. They argue that educational deprivation means the
poor don't know the best child-rearing methods; they have
never taken Psych 101, nor have their friends presented
them with copies of *What to Expect: The Toddler Years* at
their baby showers.

But these explanations shy away from the one reason
that renders others moot: poor parents raise their kids differently because they see being parents differently. They are
not simply middle-class parents *manqué*; they have their
own culture of child-rearing, and—not to mince words—
that culture is a recipe for more poverty. Without addressing that fact head-on, not much will ever change.

Social scientists have long been aware of an immense
gap in the way poor parents and middle-class parents,
whatever their color, treat their children, including during
the earliest years of life. On the most obvious level, middle-
class parents read more to their kids, and they use a larger
vocabulary, than poor parents do. They have more books

and educational materials in the house; according to *Inequality at the Starting Gate*, the average white child entering kindergarten in 1998 had ninety-three books, while the average black child had fewer than half that number. All of that seems like what you would expect, given that the poor have less money and lower levels of education.

But poor parents differ in ways that are less predictably the consequences of poverty or the absence of high school diplomas. Researchers find that low-income parents are more likely to spank or hit their children. They talk less to their kids and are more likely to give commands or prohibitions when they do talk: "Put that fork down!" rather than the more soccer-mommish, "Why don't you give me that fork so that you don't get hurt?" In general, middle-class parents speak in ways designed to elicit responses from their children, pointing out objects they should notice and asking lots of questions: "That's a horse. What does a horsie say?" (or that middle-class mantra, "What's the magic word?"). Middle-class mothers also give more positive feedback: "That's right! Neigh! What a smart girl!" Poor parents do little of this.

The difference between middle-class and low-income child-rearing has been captured at its starkest—and most unsettling—by Betty Hart and Todd R. Risley in their 1995 book *Meaningful Differences*. As War on Poverty foot soldiers with a special interest in language development, Hart and Risley were troubled by the mediocre results of the curriculum they had helped design at the Turner House Preschool in a poor black Kansas City neighborhood. Comparing their subjects with those at a lab school for the children of University of Kansas professors, Hart and Risley found to their dismay that not only did the university kids know more words than the Turner kids, they *learned faster*. The gap between upper- and lower-income kids, they concluded, "seemed unalterable by intervention by the time the children were 4 years old."

Trying to understand why, their team set out to observe parents and children in their homes doing the things they ordinarily did—hanging out, talking, eating dinner, watching television. The results were mind-boggling: in the first years of life, the average number of words heard per hour was 2,150 for professors' kids, 1,250 for working-class children, and 620 for children in welfare families.

But the problem went further. Welfare parents in the study didn't just talk less; their talk was meaner and more distracted. Consider this description of two-year-old Inge and her mother:

> Inge's mother is sitting in the living room watching television. Inge . . . gets her mother's keys from the couch. Her mother initiates, "Bring them keys back here. You ain't going nowhere."
>
> Inge drops [a] spoon on the coffee table. Her mother initiates, "O.K., now leave it alone, O.K., Inge?" . . . When she picks the spoon up again, her mother initiates, "Come here. Let me bite you if you gonna keep on meddling." Inge goes on playing; when she bangs the spoon on the coffee table, her mother initiates, "Inge, stop."
>
> . . . Inge sits on the couch beside her to watch TV and says something incomprehensible. Mother responds, "Quit copying off of me. You a copy cat." . . . Inge gets a ball and says, "Ball." Her mother says, "It's a ball." Inge says "Ball," and her mother repeats "Ball." When Inge throws the ball over by the TV as she repeats words from a commercial,

her mother responds, "You know better. Why you do that? . . . Don't throw it no more."

It's easy to spot what's wrong here. Inge's mother does not try to interest her daughter in anything—though observers noted that there were toys, including a plastic stethoscope, in the house. A different mother might pick up the stethoscope, call it by its name, pretend to use it, and invite the child to do the same. Instead Inge's mother's communication can largely be summed up by the word "no." You can't chalk this up to a lack of feeling. Hart and Risley observe that the mother is "concerned, nurturing and affectionate"; at other points in the transcript, she kisses and hugs her child, dresses her, and makes sure she gets to the bathroom when she needs to. Nor can you argue that she simply doesn't know how to engage or teach her child. Notice that she repeats the word "ball" to reinforce her daughter's learning; at other times she points out that a character on television is sleeping. But she does all this as if it were an afterthought rather than, as a middle-class mother might, one of the first rules of parenting.

In other words, Inge's mother seems to lack not so much a set of skills as the motivation to bring them to bear in a consistent, mindful way. In middle-class families the child's development—emotional, social, and (these days, above all) cognitive—takes center stage. It is the family's raison d'être, its state religion. It's the reason for that Mozart or Rafi tape in the morning and that bedtime story at night, for finding out all you can about a teacher in the fall and for Little League in the spring, for all the books, crib mobiles, trips to the museum, and limits on TV. It's the reason, even, for careful family planning; fewer children, properly spaced, allow parents to focus ample attention on each one. Just about everything that defines middle-class parenting—talking to a child, asking questions, reasoning rather than spanking—consciously aims at education or child development. In *The Family in the Modern Age*, sociologist Brigitte Berger traces how the nuclear family arose in large measure to provide the environment for the "family's great educational mission."

The Mission, as I call it, was not a plot against women. It was the answer to a problem newly introduced by modern life: how do you shape children into citizens in a democratic polity and self-disciplined, self-reliant, skilled workers in a complex economy? It didn't take all that much solicitude to prepare kids to survive in traditional, agricultural societies. That's not the case when it comes to training them to prosper in an individualistic, commercial, self-governing republic. "[I]n no other family system do children play a more central role than in that of the conventional nuclear family," Berger writes. For good reason.

Periodically social critics warn of the nuclear family's impending implosion—such as in the *New York Times* Style Section warnings about "hyperparenting" and in Judith Warner's 2005 book, only semi-hyperbolically entitled *Perfect Madness* and featured in a *Newsweek* cover story. But though future books and articles will doubtless lament the excesses of the nuclear family, though future housewives will become desperate, and though The Mission will creep into ever-new crevices of domestic life, the stubborn truth will remain that child-centeredness is the only way parents can raise successful children in our society. According to Berger, when working properly the bourgeois nuclear family is by its very definition a factory for producing compe-

tent, self-reliant, and (at its most successful) upwardly mobile children. Close the factory, as in the disappearance of
the inner-city two-parent family, and you risk shutting
down the product line.

Missionary skeptics also miss another truth. The Mission
aims at far more than promoting children's self-reliance or
ensuring that they make the soccer team or get into an impressive college. The Mission's deepest ideal is the pursuit of
happiness. In their minivan runs to swim meets and choir
practices, middle-class parents give their children a chance
to discover their talents as well as to learn the self-discipline
that makes those talents shine. In the best scenario the project leads not only to satisfying work lives but to full self-
development and self-cultivation.

The Mission aims to pass on to the next generation the
rich vision of human possibility inherent in the American
project, and to enlist them into passing down that vision to
yet another generation, in what sociologists used to call "the
reproduction of society." What goes around, comes around.

You don't have to have a Ph.D. to know that many poor
parents have not signed up for The Mission, but some academics have added to our understanding of this fact. Annette
Lareau, author of *Unequal Childhoods*—perhaps the most
extensive comparative ethnography of poor and middle-class
parents of school-age children—describes the child-rearing
philosophy among the poor and much of the working class
as "natural growth." Natural-growth believers are fatalists;
they do not see their role as shaping the environment so that
little princes or princesses will develop their minds and talents, because they assume that these will unfold as they will.
As long as a parent provides love, food, and safety, she is doing her job.

Inner-city parents are often intensely critical of their neighbors who "do nothin' for their kids," as one of Lareau's subjects puts it, but that criticism is pretty much limited to those who don't provide clean clothes or a regular dinner, or who let their kids hang out too late at night. Talking or reading to a young child or taking him to the zoo are simply not cultural requirements. Christina Wray, a Michigan nurse working with the Nurse-Family Partnership (NFP), one of the most successful programs for poor, young first-time mothers, says that when she encourages these mothers to talk to their babies, they often reply, "Why would I talk to him? He can't answer me." Mothers describe playing with or cuddling a baby or toddler, obligatory in suburban homes, as "spoiling."

Natural-growth theory also helps explain why inner-city parents don't monitor their teenagers as closely as middle-class parents do. For middle-class Missionaries, the teenager is still developing his brain and talents; if anything, his parents' obligations intensify to incorporate 6 a.m. swim practices and late-evening play rehearsals. But according to natural-growth theory, a teenager is fully grown. Dawn Purdom, one of Christina Wray's colleagues in Michigan, says that the mothers of teenage daughters she sees are more likely to look like their high school friends than their parents. "They watch TV programs together, they listen to the same music, they talk about their sexual relationships. . . . It's not like one is a leader or a role model and the other is a follower. There are no boundaries like that."

Obviously race has nothing to do with whether people become natural-growth-theory parents or Missionaries. In *Unequal Childhoods*, Lareau describes the daily ministrations of a black couple, a lawyer and a corporate manager, to their only child, Alexander, that would make Judith Warner blanch. The boy takes piano and guitar lessons, plays basketball and baseball, is in the school play and the church choir. "Daily life in the Williams house owes much of its pace and rhythm to Alexander's schedule," Lareau writes. The whole household is geared toward "developing Alexander." The first words out of both parents' mouths at the end of every day, no matter how long and stressful, are: "Have you started your homework?" or "What do you have to finish for tomorrow?" The fact that he has two married parents is an immense advantage for Alexander: together, mother and father form a kind of conspiracy to develop him, a labor-intensive and emotionally demanding project difficult enough for two parents. Lareau's sample is extremely small, but surely it is no statistical accident that all her middle-class children are growing up with their own two parents while her poor children are growing up in homes without their fathers.

You could argue, of course, that The Mission is simply too expensive for poor parents to enlist; Little League uniforms and piano lessons cost money, after all. But observers of the inner city have found numerous poor parents who seek out—and find—ways to do a lot of what middle-class parents do. They locate community centers or church groups with after-school activities. More important, they organize the household around school activities and homework. Unlike one of Lareau's poor subjects, who hardly responds when she hears that her son is not doing his homework—because "in her view it is up to the teachers to manage her son's education. That is their job, not hers"—plenty of poor parents not only pay lip service to the notion that education is important but actively "manage" their children's schooling. DePaul University professor William A. Sampson sent trained observers into the homes of a number of poor black families in Evanston, Illinois—some with high-achieving children, some with low-achieving. Although the field workers didn't go in knowing which children were which, they quickly found that the high achievers had parents who intuitively understood The Mission.

These parents, usually married couples, imposed routines that reinforced the message that school came first, before distractions like television, friends, or video games. In the homes of low achievers, mothers came home from work and either didn't mention homework or quickly became distracted from the subject. Sampson's book describes only school-age children, so we don't know how these families differed when their children were infants or toddlers; but it's a good bet that the parents of high achievers did not start showing an interest in learning only on the day their kids started kindergarten. In the ways that matter for children, these are "middle-class, lower-class families," Sampson explains in *Black Student Achievement*. "The neighborhood is not responsible for the difference. Neither is race. Neither is income." No, only the parents.

Knowing that middle-class parents better prepare kids for school, social scientists have designed an array of programs to encourage poor mothers to act more like middle-class mothers. And sometimes the programs have modest impact. In a recent survey of the literature, Jeanne Brooks-Gunn enumerates studies showing various programs that have increased maternal sensitivity, reduced spanking, "improv[ed] parents' ability to assist in problem-solving activities," and taught mothers to ask questions and initiate conversations about the books they read to their children.

Trouble is, such programs treat the parent not as a human being with a mind, a worldview, and values, but as a subject who performs a set of behaviors. They teach procedural parenting. David Burkam, a co-author of *Inequality at the Starting Gate*, explains, "The way that we [social scientists] try to make sense of the world is to break the world into small little bits and pieces and try to say which little piece is important." So they come up with a little piece that seems important and that, not coincidentally, is directly observable and measurable—like, say, discipline—and they try to find a way to teach a poor mother to reason or give a time-out rather than spank her child. They design an intervention, and they do the research to see if they have changed a mother's behavior and improved the child's situation. If the answer is yes, if there are "positive effects," the intervention is deemed a success and becomes part of the catalog of programs for improving children's chances.

But it should be clear by now that being a middle-class—or an upwardly mobile immigrant—mother or father does not mean simply performing a checklist of proper behaviors. It does not mean merely following procedures. It means believing on some intuitive level in The Mission and its larger framework of personal growth and fulfillment. In the case of poor parents, that means imagining a better life, if not for you, then for your kids. That's what makes the difference.

It is this inner parent, the human being endowed with aspiration, capable of self-betterment and of reaching toward a better future, that Bill Cosby was trying to awaken in his notorious town-hall meetings. Cosby struck many as insufficiently sensitive to the challenges that the inner-city poor face. Perhaps. But the people pouring into his lectures were not looking for sympathy. They were looking for inspiration, a vision of a better self implicit in Cosby's chastisements. This is a self that procedural parenting ignores.

No one could reasonably expect Cosby's crusade to change much on its own. But as part of a broader cultural argument from the bully pulpits of government, churches, foundations, and academia, it is essential.

5

Dads in the 'Hood

Could the black family—in free fall since the 1965 Moynihan Report first warned of the threat of its disintegration—finally be ready for a turnaround? There's sure a lot of soul-searching on the subject. A 2001 survey by CBS News and BET.com, a website affiliated with the Black Entertainment Television network, found that 92 percent of African-American respondents agreed that absentee fathers are a serious problem. In black public discourse, personal responsibility talk, always encompassing family responsibility, has been crowding out the old orthodoxy of reparations and racism. Bill Cosby's just-discussed remarks, calling on parents to take charge of their kids and for men to "stop beating up your women because you can't find a job," set off an amen corner. Democratic National Convention keynote speaker Barack Obama, the black who was to be elected Illinois senator, celebrated family, hard work, and the inner-city citizens who "know that parents have to parent." In a *New York Times* op-ed, Harvard professor Henry Louis Gates added his blessing when he asked, "Are white racists forcing black teenagers to drop out of school or have babies?" Even the wily Reverend Al Sharpton corrected one of the *New York Times*'s most fervent PC watchdogs, Deborah Solomon, that, no, Cosby wasn't being racist, and that "we didn't go through the civil rights movement only to end up as thugs and hoodlums."

A few statistics even hint that a turnaround is *already* in motion. The Census Bureau reports that between 1996 and 2002 the number of black children living in two-parent families increased for the first time since the 1960s, from 35 to 39 percent. Black teen pregnancy rates have plummeted 32 percent in the last fifteen years, well surpassing the decline among white and Hispanic adolescents. Thanks to the 1996 welfare reform bill, black mothers have joined the workforce in record numbers and made enough money to pull more of their children out of poverty than we've seen since anyone's been keeping track of these things.

And the men—the much needed husbands and fathers? You can see a glimmer of hope here too. People are talking about fathers—a lot. The *New York Times Magazine* captured the emerging dadism in Jason DeParle's August 2004 profile of a thirty-two-year-old former crack dealer, pimp, and convict trying to go straight, delivering pizzas by night, taking care of his two-year-old son by day.

But the grim fact is that bringing a reliable dad into the home of the 80 percent or so of inner-city children growing up with a single mother is a task of such psychological and sociological complexity as to rival democracy-building in Iraq. Pundits point to the staggering rates of black male unemployment and incarceration as the major reason why black men don't get married. Others cite the poisonous relations between the sexes that too often lead to domestic violence. What is little understood is that all of these—single fatherhood, domestic abuse, unemployment, crime, and incarceration—are in effect the same problem. They are all part of a destructive pattern of drift, of a tendency for men to stumble through life rather than try to tame it, a drift whose inevitable consequence is the deadbeat dad and fatherless children.

But let's start with the good news, because it is truly worth cheering. There's a fatherhood awakening under way in the inner city. According to many observers, more and more young fathers are "taking responsibility" or "stepping up" for their children. Now that post-welfare reform mothers are getting up early for the morning shift at a downtown nursing home or hotel kitchen, the men are often out there walking their kids to school, or taking them to the park or to after-school programs. "You never used to see this," says D. J. Andrews, a communications consultant who has been working with inner-city fathers for five years. "People used to say, 'That's a woman's job.'" Columbia social-work professor Ron Mincy, an expert on the inner-city family, also sees a "sea change" in hip-hop culture: it's "no longer cool" to father a child and wave from a distance occasionally. In fact some hip-hop icons are going all Ozzie, crooning their devotion and life lessons for their sons. "You a blessin' and I'll always guide you," sings rapper Ray Benzino, co-owner of *Source Magazine* and organizer of the publication's 2002 event "to reveal the nurturing side of rap artists as fathers and mentors."

Not that this celebration of fatherhood is universal in the ghetto. Andrews says that when he explains the poverty and psychological problems that fatherless children suffer at disproportionate rates, some young men say, "I never thought about that." Others listen suspiciously and counter, "I didn't have a father, and I came out okay"—that is, until Andrews points out that that's a prison record in their file, not an honor-roll certificate.

But indifference of this sort is going out of style as ghetto dwellers have begun to take stock—in their high schools, housing projects, and streets—of the disastrous results of decades of father absence. For the hip-hop generation that grew up at the height of the crack epidemic, when so many of their elders vanished into underclass hell, rage at deadbeat dads has become a kind of primal scream. In 2001, BET.com encouraged visitors to post Father's Day greetings. Organizers assumed they would see a Hallmark fest of "I love you" or "I miss you." Instead they got a "venting session": "I hate you," "To all my deadbeat dads out there, I just want to say, thanks for nothing," and "That bastard forgot that I even existed," contributors railed.

Father loss is a recurrent theme in contemporary black music, chronicled by some of the baddest brothers: "What's buried under there? / Was a kid torn apart once his pop disappeared? / I went to school, got good grades, could behave when I wanted / But I had demons deep inside," raps Jay-Z, who was raised in Brooklyn's notorious Marcy Projects and usually sings of "hos and bitches." "Now all the teachers couldn't reach me / And my mom couldn't beat me / Hard enough to match the pain of my pops not seeing me." Not everyone reacts to father loss with thuggish rage, of course—as witness Luther Vandross's sentimental Grammy Award–winning "Dance with My Father": "Then up the stairs he would carry me / And I knew for sure I was loved. . . . How I'd love, love, love / To dance with my father again."

Fatherhood is also getting a boost from a social-services industry that had long been in dad-denial. For close to half a century the welfare establishment viewed fatherlessness as poverty's unavoidable collateral damage. Federal and local governments spent billions on mom's parenting and work skills, day care and Head Start, food stamps, after-school programs, and health care; but they didn't have much to say about—or to—dad. Starting in the mid-1990s, reams of research began to convince even the most skeptical activists and policymakers of the importance of fathers and the two-parent family to children's life chances, and attention turned toward the missing dad. Today programs that try to impress young single fathers with their importance in their kids' lives are spreading across the social-services world, with support from the federal and state governments. "There's a lot of buzz about this right now," D. J. Andrews says.

Can the buzz evolve into something more than talk? The answer may strike skeptics as too pat: not unless these fathers can become husbands. But take a close look at the tenuous, improvisational, and usually polygamous relationships that replace marriage in the inner city. They're a breeding ground for confusion, resentment, jealousy, and rage of the sort that swamps the best paternal intentions.

For a good example of the shaky promise of the black fatherhood programs that do not include marriage, consider Tyrell, a soft-spoken, dreadlocked twenty-four-year-old I interviewed at a child-support work program at America Works, an employment agency for hard-to-place workers. "My generation grew up without fathers," Tyrell says. "I wanted my father—but the hell with that dude." He is determined to do better for his own nineteen-month-old son, spending hours each day with the boy and often joining with friends who are also doing the dad thing. "My friends, all our kids hang together. I'm Uncle Tyrell." Not that the young father is content to be a friendly companion. With a smile he mentions that, when the child is acting up, the boy's mother turns to Tyrell to say, "Talk to your son!"

But even though Tyrell seems to be doing much of what fathers are supposed to do—providing discipline, sharing child care, and taking at least some financial responsibility—and even though he is determined to be the father he never had, his good intentions are slender reeds in the treacherous drift of street life. As he mentions casually, he no longer lives with his son's mother; he has a new girlfriend, and their baby is due in January.

Tyrell's haphazard approach to what social scientists call "family creation" is nothing unusual. People who work closely with the men-who-would-be-fathers describe it this way: a man and woman—or perhaps a boy and girl of fifteen and sixteen—are having a sexual relationship. They're careful at first but soon get careless. (The rate of contraceptive use at first intercourse has gone up among teen girls from 65 percent in 1988 to 76 percent in 1995, but after that, a third of these girls use contraception erratically.) Sure enough, she's pregnant. In some cases he disappears on her, but more likely these days he recognizes, like Tyrell, that "he's got responsibilities." He goes to the prenatal appointments with her at the neighborhood clinic; he's there in the hospital when the baby arrives healthy and bawling, family members clap him on the back, and he's thinking, "Well, I may not have expected this, but it's pretty cool." It's what Leon Henry, head of the Maryland Regional Practitioners' Network for Fathers and Families, calls "'the happy pappy syndrome': the baby comes, and it seems like everything's wonderful."

Of course, it's not. The Accidental Father is trying to build a family without a blueprint. For one thing, he has no idea what, aside from bringing over some Huggies and Similac, he is supposed to do. After all, there weren't any fathers around when he was a child. Some men say they grew up not even being sure what to call these ghostly figures in their lives—Dad? Pops? George or Fred?—or what fathers say to their kids beyond "How ya doin'?" or "How's school?" "To me, fathers were somewhat of a luxury, an 'extra' parent of sorts," the journalist Darrell Dawsey, who grew up in a single-parent household in inner-city Detroit, explains in his memoir *Living to Tell About It.* "My father had left when I was an infant, gone down that same road of abandonment most of my other friends' fathers had taken. His idea of parenting was to fly me every few years to wherever he was living at the time and, in the guise of offering wise counsel, harangue me about the way my mother was raising me." When Dawsey's own daughter was born, he was bewildered. "I loved my daughter, but I didn't know how or why I was supposed to be there for her. I just didn't know."

But by far the biggest obstacle for the Accidental Father—and fanning his uncertainty—is his fragile, vaguely defined relationship with his baby's mother and her family. The problems don't always appear right away. At first many couples enjoy a surge of hope and good intentions. The Fragile Families and Child Wellbeing Study—following a birth cohort of nearly four thousand children of unmarried, low-income, urban parents as well as twelve hundred married couples over five years—has found that some two-thirds of inner-city single women were still romantically involved with their babies' fathers at the time of birth. When asked, a majority of these couples say they are considering marriage, and many refer to each other as "husbands" and "wives."

Still, many of these relationships will end before the child can sit up in a high chair; most will be over before he can tie his shoes. Research conducted for Head Start found that while at birth more than 80 percent of mothers and fathers are romantically involved, four years later that number has declined to 20 percent. The problem is most acute among African Americans; Fragile Families researchers found that Hispanics are two and a half times more likely to marry the year following nonmarital birth than African-American parents are.

Outsiders may find these facts troubling; young men like Tyrell do not. Having grown up in the crack-era inner city, few have ever seen a long-term partnership between a man and a woman raising children together. And without such a model, they are unlikely to see it as a goal worth pursuing. I asked Tyrell what he thought about the idea of having children with one woman with whom you stayed for good. He gave me a look of gentle condescension. "In this day and age, I don't see that happening. . . . You just do the best you can." What message would he give his own child about starting a family? "I would tell my son, 'Don't have a child until you're ready to have a child.'"

Several teens interviewed by Jason DeParle in his *New York Times Magazine* story scoff at the boring sameness of marriage, even while they yearn for fathers. "I need some little me's—children," one sixteen-year-old told DeParle, but, he continued, "I just can't see myself being with one woman." As another teen explained, "That'd be too plain—like you have to see the same woman every day." A young man with this attitude does not spend time "looking for Ms. Right" or "working on a relationship" or any of the other rituals of middle-class courtship. Like Tyrell, first he is with one woman, then he is with another; in all likelihood there will be more in the future. Sex happens. And so do babies.

It's not at all uncommon to meet poor men who have left behind a winding trail of exes and their unanticipated progeny. One man I spoke with has five children by two women. Another, apologizing for his shoddy birth-control practices by explaining that he "likes it raw," has seven children by five women; he was fifteen when the first was born. When asked about his offspring, an edgy Haitian, who owes the State of New York child support of $35,000, starts counting slowly on his fingers. He stops at four, but he doesn't seem to be joking; it's as if he's never thought of the products of his many affairs as a single group that could be labeled "my children."

Sometimes the couple is philosophical about their relationship's end. "When your woman wanna go, she's gonna go," shrugs Frank, the father of a two-year-old boy born to a mother he had lived with for five years. An amiable man, whose hardware-weight bling enhances his considerable bulk, Frank says he either sees his child or phones him every day, despite his loss of interest in the boy's mother. "I don't hate my baby's mama. She's got a interest in somebody. I got a interest in somebody. . . . No use you being miserable, her being miserable. The child gonna be miserable. . . . My son right now still has a smile on his face. Daddy's gonna live his life." After all, he had "no problem" with the two fathers of the two children his ex already had when he moved in with her. "You *know* this woman. You know she picked you. She ain't gonna pick no creep."

A lot of ghetto women voice similarly friendly feelings toward the fathers of their children and are sympathetic to their efforts to come through for them. Although their child-support relationships are usually informal—unless they are on welfare, in which case the courts set the father's contribution—the men come by when they can with money, new clothes, and Christmas presents.

But usually bitterness creeps into the relationship. The mother has special cause for resentment; she is raising a child either on her own or in a relationship with only vaguely defined obligations. One day the father arrives at the apartment and walks into what some veteran dads refer to as "mama drama"—a litany of demands and accusations, some no doubt deserved: he is late, he didn't show up last week when he said he would, he hasn't delivered the money he promised for the high chair. His girlfriend's mother, understandably mistrustful of the cause of the wailing newcomer to an already chaotic apartment, adds an unfriendly greeting of her own: this is "grandma drama." "He's eighteen, she's sixteen. He drops by to see the baby. He's got some Pampers and formula," explains Neil Tift, director of training for the National Practitioners Network for Fathers and Families. "Grandma doesn't respect him. No matter how much he wants to see the child, how much abuse is he going to take?" "Many black men say to me that the sisters are just too much work," says Nick Chiles, co-author with his wife, Denene Millner, of numerous books on the relationships of African-American men and women. Once men find themselves getting in tangles with women they think of as girlfriends, not as wives, it's no wonder.

Not all men accept the game of musical families as inevitable. Some try to live up to a dimly remembered ideal of a husbandlike partner. What are the chances they can succeed? They've stumbled into fatherhood with a woman they had not intentionally chosen to be the mother of their child; they face a future with someone with whom they share no hopes, aspirations, or trust. Ben, a handsome, serious thirty-seven-year-old dressed in a neat, blue plaid shirt, whom I also spoke with at America Works, is a poignant example of how decency and determination can be no match for the nearly insurmountable task that these men have set for themselves.

Seven years ago Ben had what he saw as a casual affair with a Dominican woman he didn't know all that well. When she needed a place to stay, he gave her his key, and one thing led to another. "I didn't expect her to get pregnant. The relationship she and I had—we had no business having children," he says sternly. Staying with her after his son was born, he tried to transform his Accidental Family into something solid and permanent. After all, he had been taught to be responsible: "My mother told me, when you make a baby, you raise a baby." And the wound of his own fatherlessness was still raw; he says he suffered "temper disorders" and problems in school because he needed the man who was never there. He wanted to give his son a childhood he never had. "I get him toys," he tells me. "When I grew up I didn't have any toys."

Ben's good intentions were not enough. Although "I begged her not to have any more children," soon she was pregnant again, with a girl this time. They broke up, got back together, broke up again, and had yet another girl. So now Ben had fathered three children with a woman he refers to as his wife, though he never married her and no longer lives with her, and though he sees her as an obstacle to his children's future. He wants the kids to go to Boys' Club or karate; she rarely takes them anywhere. He wants them to succeed in school; she shows little interest even in learning to speak English or helping the kids get ahead. I ask him again, why did he keep having children with a woman he didn't care for, much less love, and whom he viewed as a poor mother? "There's nothing wrong with wanting to be a father," he answers. "Anyone raised decently would want a kid. I know about being a man."

This theme—what it means to be a man—recurs insistently in the musings of poor black men. It has a long history, of course, stretching back to slavery and Jim Crow, when whites called black men "boy." And in the postsegregation era the indifference of the social-services establishment, policymakers, academics, and the media toward black men as fathers and husbands further undermined their sense of masculinity. Worse, enabled by welfare, women let the men know that they could manage without them; a poor black man's own children saw him as the "extra" parent, as Darrell Dawsey put it. With no role as a man of the family, he became a baffling, often threatening figure, especially to himself. In the past fifteen years, books with titles like *Speak My Name: Black Men on Masculinity*; *Are We Not Men?*; and *A Question of Manhood* have poured off the presses. Even boys are grappling with the subject: fifteen-year-old Brian Johnson told Dawsey, "That's manhood. Unless you can support your family and respect a Black woman, you are not a man."

But supporting a family that you never chose and that you are not really part of is less a path to manhood than to still more confusion and bitterness. Men often complain they feel used by their children's mothers, and valued only for their not-so-deep pockets. "She doesn't see me as a man; she sees me as an ATM," Ben complains. And not living with the children, fathers have no idea whether the mother's demands make sense. She says the kids need new jackets: should he believe her? She's lied before. One man I spoke with has a child who was conceived two weeks after he met the mother four years ago. "This accident happened," he explained, and ever since she got pregnant, she's been demanding money. "With her, it's 'F you.' It's to the point that, every time we talk, it's 'I don't want to talk. Do you got some money? That's all I want.'"

In the improvised ghetto family, the mistrust goes both ways. Patricia, a young black woman who projects an odd mixture of warmth and street toughness, lives with her two-year-old son and his father, a man she alternately refers to as her fiancé and husband, who has also fathered an older daughter he no longer sees. To protect herself and her child, Patricia hides any money she earns. "You gotta play broke," she explains. "I work for me and my son, not for my husband." Despite their seeming intimacy—she says they are talking about marriage—the couple is nothing like a parental unit. "I get scraps," she says of the money her "husband" gives her. "He sees it as 'he's helping me.'" I ask whether they would ever think of pooling their money, and she guffaws. "He thinks that's 'the white way'"—that if a man gives a woman the check, "he's an idiot." In fact, any time there's a problem and she wants to talk things over, he says, "You think you're white. Just leave it alone." She concludes about her possible husband, father of her little boy, "I think the fool is just like that. He's never going to change."

Adding to the mistrust and further threatening to isolate a father from his children is the moment when the new woman, often pregnant, enters this domestic standoff. Maybe the new girlfriend is worried that he'll favor his children by his old girlfriend. As one mother of two explained, "If a man has more than one child, the first woman gets whatever she needs, and the second child gets what's left." Maybe the first mother still carries a torch for her child's father and is jealous of his new woman. Or maybe she's worried that her child will "get scraps." Another America Works client, Randy, says his three children's mother was so convinced that his new girlfriend was getting more than she was that she has turned their children against him. "Your father's no good, no motherfuckin' good!" she screams at them. Now his nine-year-old calls him and curses him out, joining the spiteful "you're no good" chorus. Randy insists that he is providing child support. But, like many men, he complains that the money goes through the courts to the family; a father doesn't get to give it to his children with his own hands. If the mother is really determined to undermine her ex, she can (as in this case) tell their kids that he is a deadbeat.

Behind these struggles lurks the ever-present suspicion that men are lying, cheating, "low-down dogs." "Men weren't to be trusted," writes the journalist Michael Datcher, author of *Raising Fences: A Black Man's Love Story.* "Even when our mothers didn't speak these words, their tired lives whispered the message." And hip-hoppers like "I-don't-love-'em;-I-fuck-'em" Jay-Z gleefully celebrate men's treachery. According to a number of observers, wariness about cheating men is the biggest reason why inner-city women don't want to marry. And no wonder. *The Sexual Organization of the City*, a University of Chicago study of sexual relations in various Chicago neighborhoods, finds "transactional" sexual relationships, infidelity, and domestic violence on the rise throughout the city, but things are worst in Southtown, the pseudonymous African-American neighborhood. Sixty percent of Southtown men interviewed had "concurrent partners," as did 45 percent of women. The sociologist-authors conclude that polygamy is Southtown's "dominant structure."

Worse, the study's authors argue, infidelity often leads to violence. Close to 60 percent of Southtown respondents reported that at least one partner in their relationships engaged in physical violence in the previous year. The black writer bell hooks says she often hears teenagers say, "There is no such thing as love." In a relationship dystopia like Southtown, they may be right.

This social and emotional reality casts real doubt on the prevailing theory about why so few black children are born to married parents. According to that thesis, there just aren't enough stably employed men in the ghetto for women to marry. In Harvard sociologist William Julius Wilson's theory, when "work disappears" from the inner city— Wilson was referring specifically to the decline of manufacturing jobs—men do not marry since they can't support families. According to Wilson, employed, single black fathers aged eighteen to twenty-one in Chicago's inner city are eighteen times more likely to marry eventually than their jobless counterparts. More recently, pundits have updated Wilson's theory to take into account the many black men in prison. "Is there any mystery to the disintegration of the black family," Cynthia Tucker wrote not long ago in the *Atlanta Journal-Constitution*, "with so many young black fathers locked up?" Following Wilson, a recent paper from the Fragile Families Study supports what might be called "the marriage market theory." The researchers concluded that the reason that unwed black couples were less likely to marry than whites or Hispanics after having a baby was that there was an "undersupply" of employed African-American men.

The marriage market thesis makes sense as far as it goes: far too many poor black men seem like a risk not worth taking for marriage-minded women. As Northeastern University's Labor Market Studies found, in 2002 one of every four black men was idle all year long, a much greater number than whites and Hispanics—and this does not even include homeless or incarcerated men. There are only 46 employed African-American males per 100 females in the twenty cities that the Fragile Families Study observes, in contrast to 80 men with jobs in the Hispanic and white groups. Worse still, the Justice Department reports that close to 13 percent of black men are in jail, compared with under 2 percent of white men. Another estimate has it that 30 percent of noninstitutionalized black men have criminal records. More black males get their GED in prison than graduate from college. And the future does not look much better: 60 percent of incarcerated youth aged eighteen and under are African American.

But the marriage-market thesis, by emphasizing marriage as an economic relationship, understates the centrality of cultural norms about love and the way those norms organize young people's lives. Most American men take it for granted that not just marriage but the pursuit of long-lasting love is an essential life project. They spend a good deal of their adolescence and early adulthood trying to find "the one." And when they think they've found that person, they have a predictable script in mind: they imagine and plan a life with her, one that usually involves children; they assume that both of them will be faithful; they take public vows to sanctify their shared life venture. Things far too often these days don't work out the way they're supposed to, but the very existence of an inherited script endows life with meaning and orders the otherwise disconnected existence of individual men, women, and children.

But poor black men have no script to guide their deeper emotions and aspirations. Neither searching for, nor expecting, durable companionship with the opposite sex, they settle for becoming Accidental Parents and Families. When co-authors Denene Millner and Nick Chiles speak to African-American audiences about their own marriage, Millner says they are greeted with cries of cynicism: "You two don't count! You're Ozzie and Harriet in blackface! You're the Cosby show! It's a fantasy!"

Reduced to conflicted, tenuous relationships with women, poor black men are more likely to express sentiments like trust, loyalty, and lasting affection for their male friends. "With some friends, we've been friends ever since we were little. When he had trouble, I am there; when I am in trouble, he's there," one incarcerated eighteen-year-old from Omaha told Dawsey. "[I]f I had trouble with my girlfriend and we end up breaking up, I can always get another girl, but . . . it's harder to break away from your friends." (This sentiment may explain why so many men view their relationships with their sons as more important than those with their daughters; they are used to relying on "the brothers.") But the angry cries of the ghetto's fatherless children prove that this solution to the human need for lasting bonds solves little. As Orlando Patterson has written in his essay "Broken Bloodlines: Gender Relations and the Crisis of Marriages and Families Among African-Americans," blacks are "the most unpartnered and isolated group of people in America and quite possibly in the world."

Michael Datcher's *Raising Fences* perfectly captures the starkness of the contrast between the love and marriage that are central to the mainstream life project, and the consequences of their absence in the ghetto. As a child during the 1970s, Datcher was bused from a poor, single-mother home in Long Beach, California, to a middle-class white school. He visited a classmate's middle-class home and was floored. "It was a feeling of stability, comfort, and safety that touched me," he recalls. "I wanted that feeling in my life." He was similarly astonished when his friend introduced him to his father. "My parental introductions had always begun and ended with the mama because the mamas were the daddies too," he says. "Not in this house. They had real fathers here. . . . I literally could not speak."

Transformed, Datcher becomes "obsessed" with "picket-fence dreams." When he finishes college and goes to graduate school, his life is on track until he has a casual affair with a woman who becomes pregnant. Datcher is distraught at having a child with a woman he does not love, just "like every other nigga." But after another ugly twist in the story—it turns out that the child is not his—he is able to resume his search and find a woman with whom he believes he can share the "stability, comfort and safety that touched" him as a boy. Love, marriage, planning for the future: they are inextricably bound.

Then where do jobs fit into this script? The marriage market thesis has it that men who cannot find decent work in a job market that treats them so shabbily will inevitably seem inadequate marriage partners. But this argument confuses cause and correlation. What is clear from listening to men like Tyrell is that indifference toward marriage grows out of the same psychological soil as the inability to earn a decent living. Men do not get married because they have a steady job; they get married because they are *the kind of person* who can get and keep a steady job. As Datcher's story shows, the very task of looking for "the right woman" means projecting yourself into the future and taking a mindful approach to life.

One of the most striking things about talking to poor inner-city men is their sense of drift; life is something that happens to them. I asked several men where they would like to see themselves in ten years; all of them gave me a puzzled, I-never-really-thought-about-it look. Both marriage and vocation are part of the project that is the deliberate pursuit of a meaningful and connected life. To put it a little differently, to marry and to earn a steady living are to try to master life and shape it into a coherent narrative.

Ballasting this sense of drift is a hugely difficult cultural task that will take more than a generation and needs the participation of the whole culture, from Bill Cosby and the president down to the local school and church. We've known for some time that, on average, kids are better off in every way when they grow up with their married parents. The task now is to spread the word that marriage is also best for the many, many poor black men who long to be fathers.

6

The Teen Mommy Track

Some years ago, when the subject of teen pregnancy was much on policymakers' minds, I interviewed thirty or so young mothers and their boyfriends and families in New York City. In many respects it was a different era. Welfare reform was hardly a gleam in Newt Gingrich's eye. Teen pregnancy rates, at near-record levels, had barely begun an impressive decline that continues to this day. It's understandable that we've moved on.

Understandable, maybe, but not smart. The United States still has the highest teen pregnancy and birthrate in the Western industrialized world; more than 400,000 girls under 20 give birth each year in this country. Just about all these mothers are unmarried and poor. The vast majority of them will stay that way; so will their children. Over the years, experts and pundits have had any number of ways to explain our teen pregnancy problem: welfare dependency, low self-esteem, ignorance about the facts of life, poor sex education, limited access to birth control. But my conversations suggested these theories were missing something. The girls I spoke with did not lack information or values or self-regard. What separated them from middle-class teenagers was their understanding of adolescence and the life script, their view about children and marriage. In short, they were living in a different culture—or subculture, to be precise.

Take Taisha Brown, a fourteen-year-old I met in a housing project in the Bronx. When I spoke with her, Taisha was clearly thinking about having a baby. She didn't say so directly, and it wasn't going to happen right away, but she smiled coyly when I asked her. Many of her friends had babies. Her sixteen-year-old cousin had just given birth a few months before, and she enjoyed helping with the infant. "I love babies," the braided, long-legged youngster said sweetly. "They're so cute. My mother already told me, 'If you get pregnant, you won't have an abortion. You'll have the baby, and your grandmother and I will help out.'" What about school or making sure the baby had a father? "I want to be lawyer . . . or maybe a teacher. Why do I need to worry about a father? My mother raised me and my sister just fine without one."

Sociologists sometimes use the term "life script" to refer to the sense individuals have of the timing and progression of the major events in their lives. At an early age we internalize our life script as it is modeled for us by our family and community. The typical middle-class American script is familiar to most readers: childhood, a protracted period of adolescence and young adulthood required for training in a complex society, the beginning of work, and, only then, marriage and childbearing. The assumption is not merely that young adults should be financially self-supporting before they have children. They must also achieve a degree of maturity by putting the storms of adolescence well behind them before taking on the demanding responsibility of molding their own children's identity.

But for minority teens like Taisha, isolated as they are from mainstream mores, this script is unrecognizable. With little adult involvement in their daily activities and decisions, their adolescence takes on a different form. It is less a stormy but necessary continuation of childhood—a time of emotional, social, and intellectual development—than a quasi-adulthood. The mainstream rites of maturity—college, first apartment, first serious job—hold little emotional meaning for these young people. Many of the girls I spoke with said they aspired to a career, but these ambitions did not appear to arise out of any deep need to place themselves in the world. Few dreamed of living on their own. And all viewed marriage as irrelevant, vestigial.

To these girls and young women, the only thing that symbolized maturity was a baby. A pregnant teenager might refer to herself as a "woman" and her boyfriend as her "husband." Someone who waits until thirty or even twenty-five to have her first child seems a little weird, like the spinster aunt of yesteryear. "I don't want to wait to have a baby until I'm old," one seventeen-year-old Latino boy told me. "At thirty, I run around with him, I have a heart attack."

The teen mommy track has the tacit support of elders like Taisha's mother, many of whom themselves gave birth as teenagers. Even if they felt otherwise, the fact is that single mothers in the inner city don't expect to have much control over their kids, especially their sons, after age thirteen—on any matter. And, with few exceptions, the fathers of the kids I spoke with were at best a ghostly presence in their lives.

Commonly, mothers expect their older children to care for, and to socialize, younger siblings and cousins, a process that, as Ronald L. Taylor of the University of Connecticut speculates, disconnects children from adult control. Fifteen-year-old Rosie, who was carrying a child of her own, described how she had always taken care of her younger brothers, though their mother did not have a job. The youngsters started calling their sister "Mom" when she was nine.

Most adolescents are heartbreaking conformists, but kids with little parental supervision are especially vulnerable to their friends' definitions of status and style. As Greg Donaldson, author of *The Ville*, notes, the streets and projects of the inner city are dominated by kids; one sees few middle-aged or elderly adults. It's no wonder such children look to their peers from an early age for guidance and emotional sustenance. *Harper's* magazine quoted a pregnant fourteen-year-old who had been taught about birth control, abortion, and the trials of single motherhood, and who captured the spirit of this teen world: "All my friends have babies. I was beginning to wonder what was wrong with me that I didn't have one too."

In this fairy-tale setting, having a baby is a role-playing adventure. In the labor room, nurses say, younger teens sometimes suck their thumbs or grasp their favorite stuffed animal between contractions. The young mother's boyfriend, if he is still around, plays "husband"; the new baby is a doll that mothers love to dress up and take out for walks in shiny new strollers. In one high school program to discourage pregnancy, I was told, each girl had to carry around a five-pound bag of rice for a week, always keeping it in sight or paying someone to watch it. By the end of the week several girls had dressed up their bags in clothes from Baby Gap. "It's like a fashion show," said one expectant eighteen-year-old. "At least for the first two years. Then they're not so cute anymore. After that, the kids are dressed like bums."

While the girls played mother, the boys and future fathers sought sexual adventure to test their early manhood. They often bragged about their conquests, which they achieved with promises—sneakers, clothes, a ride in a nice car—and with flattery. "You know I love you, baby," they'd tell a girl. "You're so pretty." Fathering children was also a sign of manhood. A group of four disgruntled young Hispanic girls, strolling their babies down a shopping street in Brooklyn, said they had sworn off men forever and that they knew of boys who got tattooed with their children's names like bombardiers tallying hits on the sides of their airplanes. Legend among these girls had it that the occasional adventurer surreptitiously punctured a condom to outwit his reluctant conquest.

But bravado, playacting, and fashion-consciousness were not the whole story, particularly for the older adolescents I met. For many of them, a baby stirred up a love they imagined would bring meaning to their drifting lives; it became an object of romance that beckoned them away from the cynical, often brutal world in which they lived. Frank, a seventeen-year-old African-American father, waxed joyful over his six-month-old daughter, who came as a sign that he must put away childish things. "Babies don't walk, they don't talk, but they get inside you so fast. Before she was born, I was a Casanova. I didn't even know who I was with. I was hanging out all the time, doing wild things. The baby slowed me down, put the brakes on things, and made me think about my future." According to University of Pennsylvania sociologist Elijah Anderson, some mothers actually want their teenage sons to have children in the hopes they will settle down.

The early sexual activity of these unsupervised youngsters—it's not uncommon to hear of experienced eleven- and twelve-year-olds—is old news. Rape and abuse help fuel this precocity; some estimates have claimed that more than 60 percent of teen mothers have been victims, with stepfathers or mothers' boyfriends often implicated. But early sex is also part of the accepted mores of teens on the mommy track. Christie, a sixteen-year-old Latino whose tidy ponytail, shorts, white socks, and sneakers might lead one to look for a tennis racket rather than the month-old daughter she held in her arms, explained that she had her first sexual encounter two years earlier because she "was sick of being the only fourteen-year-old virgin around. I didn't really like the guy that much; I was just trying to get my friends off my back. When he started telling people, 'Oh, I had her,' I was really mad. I told everyone, 'No, I was using him.'"

Teenagers, as many can miserably recall from high school, rely on derisive name-calling to enforce conformity to their social codes. Inez, a tough, outspoken twenty-year-old from a Washington Heights Dominican family, described how her unconventional behavior was criticized in much the same way a black high achiever is accused of "acting white": "My sister and I are the only ones in my building who don't have babies. When I was younger, kids used to call me names. I never brought a boyfriend around, so they called me a lesbian. They told me I was conceited, that I thought I was better than everyone else, called me 'Miss Virgin.' I tried to stay off the streets." Elijah Anderson found that African-American boys reinforce the value of sex without emotional commitment by ridiculing those who look too enchanted as "househusbands" or "pussy whipped."

Marriage, as far as these kids were concerned, was gone, dead, an unword. Some observers, following William Julius Wilson, have suggested that this is because impoverished men with limited job prospects don't make likely husbands. But to listen to the kids themselves is to hear another theme—a mistrust of the opposite sex so profound that the ancient war between the sexes seems to have turned into Armageddon. Rap singers describe girls as "hos" (whores) or "bitches," but even some of the more modest individuals I spoke with see them as tricky Calypsos scheming to en-trap boys—a view sometimes reinforced by a boy's own husbandless mother. The thirty-five-year-old mother of an eighteen-year-old explained that she wanted him "to have his fun. I don't care who he's sleeping with. I just don't want him to be trapped." For their part, girls see boys as either feckless braggarts and momma's boys or bossy intruders. "You're cursin' at me!" mocked Stephanie, an African Amer-ican from the Bronx, when I asked her if she thought of marrying her boyfriend of two years, father of a child due this summer. "Why would I want to have some man askin' me, 'Where you goin'; what you doin'?'"

Seventeen-year-old Roberto spoke woodenly throughout our conversation as he stood dutifully next to his expectant girlfriend, who was waiting to be seen by a nurse at Methodist Hospital in Brooklyn. But when I asked if he wanted to get married, it was as if I had applied an electric shock. His eyebrows shot upward and his mouth dropped. "Married? Not until I'm thirty-five or thirty at least. You get married, the trouble starts. Marriage is a big commitment." But wasn't a child an even bigger commitment? Evidently not. "A baby is from the heart. Marriage is a piece of paper, it's official. I'll be responsible for my child, make sure I support him and visit him, but marriage . . ." He shook his head.

Stephanie planned to train to be an optician while leaving her child in the care of her mother—who, like many of these grandmothers still in their thirties, quickly shifted from anger over her daughter's pregnancy to delight over the imminent arrival of what she now calls "my baby." Like most of her sisters, when asked if she worried that a baby would get in the way of her plans, Stephanie answered emphatically, "No! Not at all!"

Of all the new or expectant mothers I spoke with, only one shrugged when I asked if she had any thoughts about what kind of work she might do. About their economic futures, most girls seemed more unrealistic than demoralized or lazy. With no parents watching over them and cracking the educational whip, and with little intellectual drive or ability to organize their adolescent urges, their career notions seemed hopelessly dreamy. Several said they wanted to be a lawyer or an obstetrician the way a four-year-old, asked what he wants to be when he grows up, answers he wants to be an astronaut.

Teenage dreaminess unchecked by adult common sense defines this never-never land as much as conformity and bravado do. Lorraine Barton, a pediatric nurse at Methodist Hospital, described a progression noted by many others in the field: "A lot of kids, and I mean boys and girls, are thrilled with having a baby. They love to dress them up and show them off; they like the baby carriages and all that stuff. But they don't seem to understand the baby will grow up. Around the time the baby begins to move around and be a separate person trying to go his own way, they lose interest. These are kids themselves, but they haven't had a chance to act like that. You can be sure they don't want to be chasing a toddler. It's also around this time that you see a lot of relationships end. The boys come around to visit, bring some Pampers, and later take the child for ice cream. But that's it." Even Frank, the chastened father of a six-month-old, said of his child: "I at least want to have a relationship with her. I want to know what's going on in her life." How could he envision anything more? He barely knew his own father.

The failure to understand the power of cultural norms over youngsters, especially norms that coincide so neatly with biological urges, created a policy world that paralleled but never quite touched the never-never land of underclass teenagers. Policymakers assume that everyone is born internally programmed to follow the middle-class life script. If you don't follow the mainstream script, it's not because you don't have it there inside you but because something has gotten in your way and derailed you—poverty, say, or low self-esteem, or lack of instruction in some technique such as birth control.

According to this view, to say that early pregnancy perpetuates poverty has it backward. Instead, wrote Katha Pollit in *The Nation*, "It would be closer to the truth to say that poverty causes early and unplanned childbearing. . . . Girls with bright futures—college, jobs, travel—have abortions. It's the girls who have nothing to postpone who become mothers." But evidence contradicts the notion that early childbearing is an automatic response to poverty and dim futures. After all, birthrates of women aged fifteen to nineteen reached their lowest point over the last century during the hard times of the depression. And in the years between 1965 and 1991, while the U.S. economy rose and fell, out-of-wedlock teen births went in only one direction—up, and steeply. Meanwhile, in rural states like Maine, Montana, and Idaho, the out-of-wedlock birthrate among African Americans remained low, not because there was less poverty but because traditional, mainstream norms held sway.

A related but also flawed theory is that a lack of self-esteem caused by poverty and neglect is at the root of early pregnancy. But the responses of the girls I spoke with were characterized more by a naive adolescent optimism than by a sad humility, depression, or hopelessness. Indeed, a study commissioned by the American Association of University Women found that the group with the highest self-esteem is African-American boys, followed closely by African-American girls.

Self-esteem has a different foundation in a subculture that, unlike elite culture, values motherhood over career achievement. To listen to some policymakers, one might think that wanting to become a lawyer or anchorwoman—and possessing the requisite orderliness, discipline, foresight, and bourgeois willingness to delay gratification—are natural instincts rather than traits developed over time through adults' prodding and example. With little sympathetic understanding of the underclass teen heart, David Ellwood, an assistant secretary of health and human services in the Clinton administration, wrote: "The overwhelming proportion of teenagers do not want children, and those who do simply cannot realize what they are in for. It is not rational to get pregnant at 17, no matter what the alternatives appear to be."

Ellwood's notion of rationality presupposed that a teenager follows the middle-class life script. This failure to understand the underclass teen's worldview led him to embrace another deep-seated but mistaken theory: that unwed teen childbearing is the result of inadequate sex education. "Teenage pregnancy is a matter of information, contraception, and sexual activity, all of which might plausibly be changed," he wrote. Most sex education curriculums, including some that "stress abstinence," rely on the same belief in a fundamentally rational teenager. They set out to train students in "decision making skills," "planning skills," or something mysteriously called "life skills." Explain the facts, detail the process, the bulb will go on, and the kids will get their condoms ready or just say no.

These approaches are not so much wrong as irrelevant, for they ignore the qualities of mind that are a prerequisite for developing complex skills. Christie told a story whose general outline I heard more than once. "I was on birth-control pills. But then I slept at my cousin's house and missed a day. I took two pills the next day. I guess that happened a few times. The nurse had told me I had to take them every day, but I couldn't." Birth control, Christie unwittingly reminds us, requires organization, foresight, and self-control, often at precisely those moments when passions are most insistent. These are qualities that even adolescents from privileged backgrounds, much less those untutored in the ways of bourgeois self-denial, are often still in the process of developing. Something far deeper than simple ignorance or lack of technical skill is at work here.

Governor Mario Cuomo took the fallacy of the underclass teenager with a bourgeois soul to its logical extreme when he remarked, "If you took a 15-year-old with a child, but put her in a clean apartment, got her a diploma, gave her the hope of a job . . . that would change everything." But it takes more than a governor's decree to transform an underclass fifteen-year-old into a middle-class adult. Many programs for teen mothers have found it necessary to teach them not only how to interview for a job but also how to shop for food, how to budget money, how to plan a menu, even how to brush their teeth. Programs like these point to the devilishly tricky problem of resolving the tension between the mainstream and underclass life scripts.

Moreover, instead of discouraging unwed teen pregnancy, such programs often end up smoothing it into an alternative lifestyle. If Taisha Brown becomes pregnant, she will be able to leave her dull, impersonal school for a homey, nurturing middle school for pregnant girls like herself. Later she will very likely find a high school with a nursery where she can stop by between classes and visit with her baby, attend parenting classes, receive advice about public assistance, and share experiences with other teen mothers in counseling groups. Kathleen Sylvester, formerly of the Progressive Policy Institute, who visited such a school in Baltimore, says it is far nicer than ordinary public schools. "It's cheerful, warm; you get hugs and lots of attention." These programs were introduced with the best of intentions—to ensure that teen mothers would continue their education. But because of them it will seem to Taisha that the world around her fully endorses early motherhood.

All the prevailing analyses of teen childbearing, both liberal and conservative, neglected a troubling truth apparent throughout most of human history: nothing could be more natural than a sixteen-year-old having a baby. But in complex societies such as our own, which require not just more schooling but what the great German sociologist Norbert Elias calls a longer "civilizing process," the sixteen-year-old, though physically mature, is considered an adolescent, a late-stage child, unready for parenthood. This quasi-childhood constitutes a fragile limbo between physical maturation and social or technical competence, between puberty and childbearing, one that requires careful ordering of insistent, awakening sexual urges. This century's gallery of juvenile delinquents, gangs, hippies, and teen parents should remind us of the difficulty of this project. Even now, social workers report seeing fourteen- and fifteen-year-old wives from immigrant Albanian and Yugoslavian families coming to pregnancy clinics. The truth is that adolescent childbearing was commonplace even in the staid 1950s, when a quarter of all American women had babies before the age of twenty, though of course almost always within wedlock.

But two related social changes occurred in the late 1960s: early marriage came under suspicion, and the sexual revolution caught fire. This meant that the strategies societies generally use to control the hormonal riot of adolescence—prohibiting sex entirely and encouraging marriage within a few years of puberty—both became less workable. The "shotgun wedding" became a thing of the past. As a result, American adolescence became longer, looser, more hazardous.

Adolescents at the bottom of the socioeconomic ladder were most harshly affected by these changes. Middle-class kids have more adult eyes watching over them during this precarious period. They also have numerous opportunities for sublimation—a useful Freudian term unfortunately banished along with its coiner from current intellectual fashion—of their urges: sports teams, church or temple groups, vacations, and camp, not to mention decent schools. Their poorer counterparts don't get that attention. It's much less likely that someone watches to see whom they're hanging out with or whether they've done their homework. Their teachers and counselors often don't even know their names. And "solutions" like contraceptive give-aways and decision-making-skill classes only ratify their precocious independence.

Far better would be programs that recognized and chan-neled the emotional demands of adolescence—intensive sports teams or drama groups, for instance, which simulta-neously engage kids' affections and offer constructive, su-pervised outlets for their energies. According to some teachers who work closely with pregnant teens, births go up nine months after summer and Christmas vacation—further evidence of adolescents' profound need for struc-ture and direction.

Given that unwed early childbearing is so common for a significant subset of American society, the salient ques-tion is not why so many girls are having babies but what prevents some of their peers from following this path? I ex-plored that question with a group of five young black and Latino women in their twenties, all of whom had grown up in neighborhoods where the teen mommy track was com-mon. All were college students or graduates acting as peer AIDS counselors for teens in poor areas of the city. None had children. All but one grew up with both parents; the other was the product of a strict Catholic education in Aruba. If the meeting hadn't been arranged by the New

York City Department of Health, I might have suspected a family-values agenda at work.

All of these young women said their parents, in addition to loving them, watched and prodded them. "My father used to come out on the street and call me inside," Jocelyn recalled, laughing. "It was so embarrassing, I just learned to get in there before he came out." Intact families seem to provide the emotional weight needed to ballast the increasingly compelling peer group. Clearly, two parents are vastly better than one at keeping the genie of adolescent pregnancy inside the bottle.

These experiences jibe with both common sense and research. Asians, who have strong families and the lowest divorce rate of any ethnic group (3 percent), also have the lowest teen pregnancy rate (6 percent). In one longitudinal study, the sociologist Frank Furstenberg of the University of Pennsylvania periodically followed the children of teen mothers from birth in the 1960s to as old as twenty-one in 1987. His findings couldn't have been more dramatic: kids with close relationships with a *residential* father or long-term stepfather simply did not follow the teenage mommy track. One of four of the 253 mostly black Baltimoreans in the study had a baby before age nineteen. But *not one* who had a good relationship with a live-in father had a baby. A close relationship with a father not living at home did not help; indeed, those children were more likely to have a child before nineteen than those with little or no contact with their fathers.

A number of social critics have insisted on the profound importance of fathers in the lives of adolescent boys. But for girls a father is just as central. Inez, one of the peer AIDS counselors, said she always bristled on hearing boys boast of their female acquaintances, "I can do her anytime," or "I had her." Any woman who had grown up in a home with an affectionate and devoted father would be similarly disapproving. Having had a firsthand education of the heart, a girl is far less likely to be swayed by the first boy who attempts to snow her with the compliments she may never have heard from a man: "Baby, you look so good," or "You know I love you."

The ways of love, it seems, must be learned, not from decision-making or abstinence classes, not from watching soap operas or, heaven forbid, from listening to rap music, but through the lived experience of loving and being loved. Judith S. Musick, a developmental psychologist with the Ounce of Prevention Fund, explained that through her relationship with her father, a girl "acquires her attitudes about men and, most importantly, about herself in relation to them." In other words, a girl growing up with a close father internalizes a sense of love, which sends up warning signals when a boy on the prowl begins to strut near her.

Further, a girl hesitates before replacing the attachment she has to her own father with a new love. I recently watched a girl of about twelve walking down the street with her parents. As she skipped along next to them, busily chattering, she held her father's hand and occasionally rested her head against his arm. The introduction of a serious boyfriend into this family romance is unlikely to come soon. Marian Wright Edelman's aphorism once received wide currency: "The best contraceptive is a real future." It would have been more accurate to say, "The best contraceptive is a real father and mother."

During the waning years of the twentieth century, marriage disappeared in the inner city and faded in working-class communities. That's not what was happening in the suburbs, in the new exurbs, and in gentrified urban neighborhoods. There, marriage was making a comeback. From one vantage point, this seems surprising. For those who lived through them, the sexual and social revolutions of the late 1960s and '70s made traditional marriage seem discretionary, at best a dish on life's groaning buffet that would appeal to a few, but certainly not many, diners. Feminists in particular questioned its appeal in a "progressive" society. In the eyes of many feminists, marriage and children limited women's career success and prevented them from the adventure and self-exploration that seemed men's privilege.

But from the vantage point of those who were children through the 1960s, '70s, and '80s, when these ideas were at their zenith, the matrimonial revival is not so startling. Where social revolutionaries had promised more freedom, the children of those years experienced troubled parents, disordered homes, and diminished prospects. Feminist professors might continue to scowl at bourgeois marriage, but their young students longed for the stable homes their generation had been denied. They judged that marriage, for all its contradictions in an individualistic age, offered the best chance for deep bonds, for rootedness—and, most of all, for the rearing of successful children.

7

The End of Herstory

When you ask young women today if they think of themselves as feminists, more often than not they will pause for a moment. Then they will answer something like: "Well, I believe in equal pay for equal work," or "Yes, I do believe women should have choices," or "Of course, I believe women should have equal rights."

If these are the principles that define feminism, then we are all feminists now. And the future belongs to feminism, too: a 2001 *American Demographics* survey of adolescent girls entitled "The Granddaughters of Feminism" found that 97 percent believe women should be paid equally while 92 percent believe "lifestyle choices" should not be limited by sex. Curiously, the war on terror has, if anything, solidified our commitment to women's rights, though orthodox feminists opposed it as another dangerous example of "the cult of masculinity." The sight of women forced to scurry about in sacks brought home to Americans just how much they treasured their freedoms, including those won for women over the past decades. For a remarkable moment, President Bush and Eleanor Smeal of the Feminist Majority, which had long tried to bring Taliban mistreatment of women to the State Department's attention, seemed members of the same party—which, seen against the backdrop of radical Islam, they actually are.

But how do we explain the pause that comes when you ask women if they consider themselves part of the movement? The truth is, very few Americans are capital "F" Feminists. Polls show that only about a quarter of women are willing to accept the label. Younger women seem no more comfortable with the title than their grandmothers were. Marie Wilson, president of the *Ms.* Foundation for Women, has admitted that the elite young women who twenty years ago would have been the generals of the movement are feminists "by attitude . . . [but] are not interested in hearing about organized movements or activism." They mostly do not join NOW or read *Ms.* magazine. They don't think of themselves as second-class citizens of the patriarchy, or follow "women's issues" in the news, and their marital status seems more likely to predict how they will vote than their sex.

Activists who try to make sense of these young feminists who are not Feminists conclude that the movement has an image problem. The reason so many people believe in feminist goals yet reject the label, they say, is that the media have given us a cartoon picture of liberationists as humorless, Birkenstock-wearing man-haters, our era's version of the old-fashioned spinster. Feminism is still an "unfinished revolution," they say, and young women share its goals. They just don't like the packaging.

But this explanation falls far short. Feminism is not simply suffering from a P.R. problem. It's just over. As in *finished*.

Supporters will smile and reply that the movement has been read its last rites often during its lifetime. What's different now, though, is that feminism appears not so much dead as obsolete. Yes, it has bred a generation of empowered young women. But rooted in a utopian politics that longs to transcend both biology and ordinary bourgeois longings, it cannot address the realities of the lives that it has helped to change. Young women know this, even if their mothers do not.

Until recently, Amanda Laforge could have served as a poster girl for *Ms.* After graduating from Boston University, she went to American University's law school. When she married she kept her maiden name and her job with the Maryland secretary of state. When she got pregnant, she continued commuting forty-five minutes to her new job at the state attorney general's office. When the baby came, she planned to take three months' maternity leave, then return to the office for a continued climb up the career ladder.

It didn't turn out that way. Instead of becoming Super Career Mom, she quit her job. Yet she shows no symptoms of Oppressed Housewife Syndrome. Isn't she bored? "No. I love it." Does she miss her job? "I do miss working—or at least having colleagues. I've started to look for part-time work." Does she worry that she is not her husband's equal? "I feel superior to my husband," she sniffs. "Women are much more powerful." But won't her career suffer? "I'm struggling with this personally right now. I know I've already compromised my ability to reach the height of my career. But I see a lot of room to make up." Is it so easy to put aside your career? "No, but I had friends whose mothers were career women who just got caught up in something. Now they've worked for twenty-five or thirty years for X company, and they didn't get to such enormous heights. Would their lives have been that much different if they had worked part time? I know a lot of fairly educated people," Amanda concludes, "and no one is looking for more time at the office."

It would be a big mistake to see Amanda as a return to 1950s milk-and-cookies motherhood or as evidence of the backlash that Feminists announce with every article by Katie Roiphe. It would be equally wrong to conclude that most young mothers today are quitting work to be with their babies. Many are; but many others are working part time, or two days a week at the office, say, and three at home. And, yes, many others are going back to work full time.

But regardless of how they arrange their lives, women like Amanda illustrate a truth that feminism never anticipated and is still busily denying: after the revolution, women want husbands and children as much as they want anything in life. It's not that the daughters and granddaughters of feminism don't respect those who forgo marriage and motherhood: in the *American Demographics* poll, 89 percent of adolescent girls said a woman does not need a man to be a success, and the percentage of single women between thirty-five and forty-four has increased significantly since 1960. But the vast majority of young women continue to tell pollsters that they want to marry and have children, and they go on to do so. Census experts predict that upward of 90 percent of today's young women will eventually marry, which means, remarkably enough, that women today tie the knot at a rate similar to that of their grandmothers. Moreover, even with the widely publicized decline in fertility in recent decades, a large majority of women will also become mothers; as of 2000, 81 percent of women aged forty to forty-four had given birth to at least one child.

After giving birth, moreover, not many embrace the one preferred Feminist solution to liberated motherhood: dropping the baby off at the day-care center for fifty hours a week. According to another *American Demographics* study, having come from broken or latchkey homes, most Gen Xers think the best arrangement is for one parent to stay home with the kids, a belief that other polls suggest the majority of Americans share. This usually means mom, even after three decades of feminism and a concerted effort to get fathers to man the nursery. A 1996 Census Bureau report shows that 42 percent of children under five have a parent at home full time, another 19.4 percent part time—and the large majority of these parents are women. The latest Census Bureau numbers show that 55 percent of women with infants were in the workforce in 2000, compared with 59 percent two years earlier—the first such decline since 1979.

It's no wonder that Feminists have a hard time accepting that trends like these could represent what women actually want. After all, Feminists of the 1960s and '70s took to the streets on the premise that women wanted to escape from the prison house of the bourgeois home and take up positions in the office and the boardroom, where the real power lies. Women consigned to the role of housewife and mother measured out their days with baby spoons and dirty socks, but work, it seemed to these followers of Betty Friedan, would give them adventure, self-expression, freedom. In the seventies the offices of *Ms.* and other feminist organizations sported signs proclaiming WOMEN WORKING!

Echoes of this kind of thinking still resound in aging Feminist circles. In her book *Flux*, for example, Peggy Orenstein explains that work or career "requires the assertion of self," whereas in wifehood and motherhood "your whole identity as a person gets swallowed up." In the same vein, several years ago a successful screenwriter of about fifty told me she was contemplating divorce. When I expressed sympathetic alarm, she hastened to explain that there was nothing wrong with her marriage; it was just that "I hate that word 'wife.' It's not who I am."

Such talk has about as much resonance as "Remember the Maine!" for younger women. For one thing, the romance of work—what might be called the Feminist mystique—has faded. Young women, as more than one I interviewed put it, are far more likely to feel pressure to be "super career women" than to play Ozzie's Harriet. That doesn't mean that those fortunate enough to have challenging jobs don't take great pride in their accomplishments or enjoy the intellectual stimulation they get at the office. And it doesn't mean that there aren't plenty of young women as fiercely ambitious as Duddy Kravitz. But many are put off by the single-minded careerism they associate with feminism. In *Feminist Fatale: Voices of the Twentysomething Generation Explore the Women's Movement*, Paula Kamen interviewed a number of such skeptics. "There are many women in this field in their late thirties who don't have a family and their entire social life revolves around the job and people [on the job]," says one twentysomething. "I think that's horrible."

Remember also that most women in their twenties and thirties watched their own mothers go to work but didn't see adventurers and heroines. They saw tired women complaining about their bosses and counting the days until the next vacation, just as women their mothers' age saw their fathers doing. And they know from personal experience that taking a meeting with a client or lunching with colleagues involves every bit as much of the role-playing that Feminists wanted to escape. "I worked sixty hours a week from the time I got out of college till I got pregnant," one Boston-area thirty-year-old marketing executive said. "I was tired of it. My job is not emotionally fulfilling. I like it, but it's just a job."

In short, for these women the personal is not political—it's, well . . . personal. Even the most ambitious young women refuse to judge the housewife as, in Betty Friedan's words, a "waste of human self." Sara Ely Hulse, a recently married twenty-six-year-old CBS producer proud of her "independent nature," would seem a logical candidate for Feminist skepticism toward housewifery: her career is so promising that she and her husband consider appointing him the main caregiver when they have children. But when I asked whether she looked down on her mother, who had stayed at home to raise her and her two sisters, she answered heatedly: "Oh God, no! I loved having someone to come home to every day." A young D.C. lawyer-mother I interviewed, though she went back to work three months after giving birth, is also entirely sympathetic to stay-at-homes. After all, when she gets together with friends, she says, "All we talk about is our babies."

Nothing illustrates this reclaiming of the personal more clearly than the Mrs. question. For sixties Feminists, becoming Mrs. John Smith epitomized both women's second-class status and their economic and psychological dependence on men. Indeed, former NOW president Patricia Ireland wrote in her memoir, *What Women Want*, that a woman taking her husband's name "signifies the loss of her very existence as a person under the law." Pshaw, younger women say; it doesn't mean anything of the sort. You can keep your name if you want—and many women do, as often for practical as for philosophical reasons. You can hyphenate your name or use your maiden name for work and your married name everywhere else. Or if you want to have the same name as your husband and children, go for it. "A lot of women in my office said keeping your maiden name is a hassle, like when the school calls, or the kids' doctor, and asks for you using the child's last name," the independent-minded Sara Hulse said. "I hate hyphenated names—so I changed my name." The D.C. lawyer explained that her decision to use her husband's name was prompted by her experience growing up with a divorced and remarried mother. "I had a different name from my mother," she recalls, "and it always bothered me."

Single women, especially those in their later twenties and early thirties, have other reasons to feel impatient with the Feminist mystique. They followed the careerist script to a tee: they worked until 10 p.m., got flashy jobs, fought for promotions. Meanwhile they had sex when they felt like it, indifferent to whether their partner was husband material or not; they lived with their boyfriends, shrugged when that didn't work out, and moved on to the next one. But after some years of this, many are surprised to find that the single life is less like *Sex and the City* than like *The Apartment*.

"Sex is an easily attainable, feminist-approved goal, one that carries less stigma than admitting to loneliness or desperately wanting emotional connection with a man," writes Katherine Marsh in a *Washington Monthly* article, in one of several youthful critiques of feminism that have appeared in recent years. "While feminists can solidly advise on how to get rid of a man—obtaining a fair divorce or a restraining order against an abusive spouse—it's fairly mute on how to find love and live with a decent man." Vanessa Grigoriadis, writing in *New York Magazine*, tells of a woman whose parents, in thrall to the feminist career mystique, refused to pay for a wedding if she married before thirty. But now she and her peers are feeling uneasy. "These days, the independence that seemed so fabulous—at least to those of us who tend to use that word a lot—doesn't anymore."

These younger women are especially peeved that, in promoting female independence, feminism denied biological realities that now loom large. Feminists often like to talk about the "click"—the moment when a woman experiences discrimination so clearly that she sees her whole life in a radically new light. For a lot of younger women, the "click" moment has now arrived in a totally unexpected form. With the torrent of media coverage that followed the publication of Sylvia Ann Hewlett's *Creating a Life*—publicity that focused on the fertility problems of older high-achieving women—everything looked different. For just as there are no atheists in foxholes, there are no Feminists in the throes of fertility anxiety.

"I'm twenty-eight and grew up in Manhattan, attended a competitive private high school and a liberal-arts college," marvels Grigoriadis, "and at no point did anyone bring up the notion that the sexes were anything but equal. To me, it seemed like ideology was going to triumph over biology."

The "unwillingness to confront the personal—more precisely the feminine personal—is the biggest failure of the Second Wave," Sarah Blustain, a thirtysomething editor at *The New Republic*, has written. ("Second Wave" feminism is sixties and seventies feminism; First Wavers were the suffragettes.) "It's why the movement has refused to deal with the fact that even *after* the Revolution, many women want to marry men and bear their children. . . . It's why *Time* ran on its cover another installment of the Baby vs. Career story that drove women I know to tears for reminding us of the incredible double bind."

Even young women who embrace the Feminist label have a beef with sisterly avoidance of "the feminine personal." Susan Jane Gilman, author of *Kiss My Tiara: How to Rule the World as a Smartmouth Goddess*, is one of feminism's more dutiful daughters in many ways—her pet issues include abortion rights, sexual harassment, and domestic violence—yet she says: "For women today, feminism is often perceived as dreary. As elitist, academic, Victorian, whiny, and passé." Young women Gilman's age don't remember the thrill of the bra-burning, let's-do-it-in-the-road seventies; instead they went to the thin-lipped, Catherine MacKinnon school of feminism, where they learned that even their younger brothers were potential harassers, even rapists. They're having none of it. Calling themselves girlie feminists, lipstick feminists, or sometimes just Third Wavers, they have taken to flaunting the very femininity that Feminists had scolded would lead men to objectify them.

If there is a beauty myth, these renegades are true believers. They want their lip gloss, their Victoria's Secret lingerie, and their MTV. Then Oxford student Chelsea

Clinton, pictured in 2002 cuddling with her boyfriend in a Venetian gondola and at a Paris fashion show with a deep décolletage and enough mascara to paint a fence, looked like a girlie feminist. At her age, her mother sported geeky glasses and unkempt hair, emblems of the I've-got-more-important-things-on-my-mind-than-attracting-a-man branch of feminism, the Second Wave incarnate.

Still, it is more than nail polish that makes these daughters very different from what their mothers envisioned when they groomed them to take over the family business. For all their in-your-face sexual bravado, girlie feminists can be unabashed traditionalists. Consider *Bust*, a girlie Internet 'zine that describes itself as "the magazine for women with something to get off their chests." With its signature T-shirts that say KISS MY ASS and TOUGH TITTIES, and its pronouncement of "The New Girl Order," *Bust* is full of Erica Jongish, zipless-sex Attitude. Yet as the title of one article, "A Bad Girl's Guide to Good Housekeeping," suggests, the hipness coexists with more conventional desires. A recent chat-room offering, "A Feminist Analysis of the Baby Scare," was less MacKinnon than *Bride*. "I'm conflicted," one participant wrote. "Did some feminists drop the ball on this one? Have we understated the power of biology?" Another contributor was just mad: "I am not a mother and I am still not sure if/when I will be one," she wrote. "But it really depresses me that if I do choose to get knocked up before the age of 30, that I will be looked upon as nothing more than a tool of the patriarchy. Sisterhood is powerful. Baloney."

What all this suggests is a vast and sharper-than-a-serpent's-tooth generation gap between Feminists and their progeny. "A woman in her twenties or thirties and I are in parallel universes, as if we were in two different countries,"

Gloria Steinem has admitted. Being the out-of-touch old-timers is especially painful for aging boomer-Feminists, once so proud of being in the vanguard. In the course of researching her 1999 memoir of the women's movement, *In Our Time*, Susan Brownmiller looked up many old activist acquaintances and found them "very depressed" at their irrelevance. Other Second Wavers get prickly: how can these youngsters be so ignorant of what is at stake here?

Lisa Belkin, a *New York Times* reporter who covers the "work/life" beat and frequently recounts her own attempts to balance her enviable career with two young sons and a husband, was once on the receiving end of this irritability, when Maureen Corrigan, a boomer Georgetown literature professor, reviewed her new collection of columns, *Life's Work*. Corrigan blasted the younger woman's failure to show more respect for the Second Wave legacy. Where Belkin cheerfully accepts the inevitable tensions between her career and family life, Corrigan spies the "small pathologies of an unfinished revolution." Where the frankly ambitious Belkin nevertheless acknowledges that the stresses of her husband's job as a pediatric cardiologist make her own deadline pressures seem less intense, Corrigan frets that young women should "stop apologizing for having professional ambitions and minds of their own." And when Belkin describes the confusion that sometimes comes from using her maiden name at work and her husband's name socially, Corrigan explodes: this young woman has a "weirdly reactionary split personality," she snarls. "Why [did] she choose to create problems for herself by taking her husband's last name in the first place?"

Meanwhile the younger generation concludes that older women just don't get it. Peggy Orenstein, who in her late thirties is old enough to be a card-carrying member of the Sisterhood but young enough to know that the future needs attending to, traveled around the country asking two hundred women about their attitudes toward work, romance, and family for her 2001 book *Flux*. She was puzzled to find women who share neither her passion for work nor her ambivalence toward marriage and motherhood. During the question period after a speech at Washington University, a student burst out: "I don't want to have to wait until I'm thirty-five to have kids!" Orenstein's priceless reaction speaks volumes about the chasm between the New Girl Order and the Second Wave Old Guard. "I nodded too, sympathetically. It really wasn't fair. Then suddenly, I thought, 'Wait a minute! I'm nearly thirty-seven and I don't have children yet. These women don't want to be *me*.'"

Of course, many older Feminists are shocked—*shocked!*—that their daughters' generation could think that they looked down their noses at the feminine personal. "The notion that the women's movement denigrates women who choose the traditional roles of wife and mother is arrant nonsense," columnist Molly Ivins writes emphatically. She might want to sign up for a few women's studies classes at Yale or the University of Texas or check out the current literature from NOW. What she'll find is not just hostility to "traditional roles" but a tight-wound ambivalence toward the biological urges that young women now so loudly affirm and a hostility to bourgeois life that few young women share.

Take the Feminist attitude toward marriage. When college women sit at the knee of their female elders, they may well read from the widely used textbook *Women's Realities, Women's Choices*. There they will learn that "the institution of marriage and the role of 'wife' are intimately connected with the subordination of women in society in general." For the teachers, this attitude isn't just theoretical. Daphne Patai, co-author of *Professing Feminism* and author of *Heterophobia*, books critical of the women's studies industry, recounts a lunch with other female academics at which one announces she is getting married. The response: shocked, dead, embarrassed silence.

Yet Feminist hostility to marriage goes beyond the view that it makes women second-class citizens. Feminists also cling to the ideal of the postbourgeois, liberated woman who not only doesn't need a man but also rejects conventional middle-class life in favor of a self-created, adventurous independence. When Gloria fish-without-a-bicycle Steinem married in 2000, for example, she evidently felt she had to lend her act a heroic, anti-bourgeois cast. "I had no desire to get married and neither did he," she said—but "it seems rebellious at 66."

Motherhood too interests orthodox Feminists only insofar as it overturns bourgeois norms. NOW, for example, fiercely supports single welfare mothers and bristles at any reform that might try to encourage them to go to regular jobs or—God forbid—to marry. Ireland got herself arrested at a 1996 demonstration at the Capitol when the House passed "the Republican welfare bill that would have plunged millions of women and children deeper into poverty," as she put it in her memoir. Although child poverty and overall poverty have declined since welfare reform, NOW has failed to acknowledge its error. In addition, the group continues to sound the alarm against current proposals to promote marriage. As Kim Gandy, the current NOW president, says, the plan reminds her of her backward "grandmother's friends say[ing], 'Honey, when are you going to get married?'"

Still, the NOW folks can believe in the happily-ever-after—as long as they're talking about lesbians. NOW heavily promotes gay marriage and adoption—not, like other advocates, as a civil rights issue but because they view lesbian liaisons and motherhood as a means of subverting conventional marriage and sex roles. Author and journalist Norah Vincent, a gay libertarian, dismisses the organization's support. "It's the old Marxist agenda. Feminists see gay people as the newest proletariat. They want to overthrow the old bourgeois system. It's not my agenda." She adds that she and her girlfriend often joke that they would love nothing more than a traditional middle-class life. "We think of advertising: 'Two women willing to do housework and take care of children in return for a husband.'"

But while Feminists can get as misty as a Hallmark card over lesbian and welfare mothers, they cast a colder eye upon the other 90 percent of women who might look longingly inside Snuglis and baby carriages. Phyllis Chesler, author of the Second-Wave best-seller *Women and Madness*, recounts that when she became pregnant in the late seventies, friends begged her not to have a child, which would cause her to abandon the movement. These days, when faced with young female baby hunger, Second Wavers are still acting as skittish as Hugh Hefner. In the fall of 2001, for example, alarmed at infertility problems they were seeing in the increasing number of women putting off childbearing into their forties, the American Society for Reproductive Medicine launched an ad campaign warning that "Advancing Age Decreases Your Ability to Have Children." But where the doctors were focusing on the gap they observed between medical fact and wishful thinking on the part of contemporary women, one that had already brought many to grief, the Feminists spied only the ever-lurking bourgeois backlash against the heroic career woman. "There is an antifeminist agenda that says we should go back to the 1950's," Caryl Rivers, a professor of journalism at Boston University and a frequent commentator on Feminist issues, pronounced in *Time*. "The subliminal message is 'Don't get too educated; don't get too successful or too ambitious.'"

And here we come to the primary reason for feminism's descent into irrelevance. Whereas most young women will at some point want babies like they want food, for Feminists, motherhood is the ten-ton boulder in the path of genuine liberation. It mucks up ambition, turning fabulous heroines of the workplace—killer lawyers, 24/7 businesswomen, and ruthless senator wannabes—into bourgeois wifies and mommies. It hinders absolute equality since women with children don't usually crash through glass ceilings. They resist traveling three days a week to meet with hotshot clients; they look at their watches frequently and make a lot of personal phone calls.

Nothing irks a movement Feminist more than news of a Sister packing in a high-powered career. Candice Carpenter, who when she married left her position as CEO of iVillage, changed her name, and joined the ranks of stay-at-home mothers, earned the wrath of Brandeis professor Linda Hirshman, who called her "the born-again Stepford wife." When presidential aide Karen Hughes announced that she was leaving Washington because her family was "homesick" for Texas, Hirshman was equally incensed, blasting Hughes's husband for not "supporting her career" and for failing to promote "justice in the private world of the family."

Feminists deal with the unsettling fact that, even after the revolution, women persist in wanting to be mothers in two ways. The first tack is simple denial. Amazingly, given young women's preoccupation with how to balance work and motherhood, neither NOW nor the Feminist Majority, the movement's two most influential organizations, includes maternity leave, flex time, or even day care on its list of vital issues.

The other tack, favored by academic Feminists, is a more complex denial. Yes, women may want babies, they concede; but that doesn't mean they want motherhood—at least not motherhood as it has been "constructed" by the patriarchy throughout history. For these theorists, only a social arrangement that makes men and women exactly equal co-parents—at work precisely the same number of hours, and taking care of the children precisely the same number of hours—is acceptable. In a 2002 article in *The American Prospect*, Janet Gornick averaged out the number of hours worked by mothers of children under three (23) and those worked by fathers (44) and proclaimed the egalitarian goal: both mom and dad should work 33.5 hours a week. It is not enough to give men and women more flexibility and choices about how to organize their lives; the goal is "unbending gender," as American University law professor Joan Williams puts it in her book of that title. Williams rejects what she calls "choice rhetoric"; a woman who thinks she is freely choosing to stay home is just fooling herself, in thrall to the "ideology of domesticity."

Feminists who share Williams's and Gornick's goals aren't about to let biology get in the way of their plans for utopian parity. Although they don't go as far as those 1970s radicals who looked forward to growing fetuses outside the womb, they search for ways to make every aspect of motherhood a fifty-fifty proposition. In *Woman: An Intimate Geography*, for instance, Natalie Angier comes up with one idea about "sharing" breast-feeding: if the father would just rock the baby between feedings "against his naked breast," men too could have "a visceral connection with a newborn."

Little wonder that few women in their twenties and thirties seek to complete this so-called unfinished revolution. They don't yearn for the radical transformation of biological restraints and bourgeois aspirations devoutly wished by stalwarts. Even those few who want more androgynous sex roles for themselves don't wish to impose them on others. Yes, they took women's studies courses—often only to satisfy their colleges' diversity requirements—but they came away unimpressed. To many of them, feminism today represents not liberation but its opposite: a life that must be lived according to a strict, severe ideology. The younger generation, on the other hand, wants a liberation "that isn't just freedom to choose [but] . . . freedom from having to justify one's choices," as Jennifer Foote Sweeney has put it in *Salon*. In short, they're ready to depoliticize the personal.

But none of this means that the second sex is entirely at peace in the New Girl—or the New Woman—Order. There is a deep tension between young family values and female ambition that will spark many years of cultural debate—and it's not just about who's going to do the laundry or take the kids to the pediatrician. There is still plenty of grumbling on that score, of course: in her 2002 study *For Better or for Worse*, for example, Mavis Hetherington found that two-thirds of married women complained about the disproportionate burden of house and child care that falls on their shoulders (though she also found that traditional families, with breadwinner husband and stay-at-home wife, had the lowest rate of divorce).

But more important, biology simply disagrees with our careerist culture. The evidence is that, even after thirty years of the Feminist mystique, women may want men to help out more, but they still want to be the primary parent and nester-in-chief. *The Motherhood Report*, a 1989 survey of more than one thousand mothers, found that while three-quarters of women want men to pitch in more, their goal is not fifty-fifty parenting. They like being boss at home. Suzanne Braun Levine's 2000 *Father Courage: What Happens When Men Put Family First* suggests that in this department not much has changed in the past ten years. Levine went searching for "the second stage of the gender role revolution"—couples who defy all traditional mommy-daddy divisions. She found some who, with much struggling, were doing so (though you don't have to be Robert Young to think that her description of the brutal, dawn-to-midnight, pass-the-baton existence of some of her couples—think of it as X-treme domesticity— makes *Father Knows Best* look like a sane alternative). But she also finds, contrary to the Feminist picture of the patriarchy foisting unwanted roles on women, that it is often the second sex who, wanting to be the first sex in the nursery, undermines these arrangements.

In my own interviews I found that young women are not especially nervous about thinking of this stubborn clinging to traditional roles as based in biology. When you ask if there are innate differences between the sexes, they talk comfortably in some of the terms that would satisfy an evolutionary psychologist. They generally believe that women have a closer bond with babies. They see that women usually play what one thirtyish lawyer called "household executive." And they're not especially worried about it. "I don't see it as injustice unless [women] are denied opportunity," one lawyer shrugged. As Norah Vincent concludes, "Equal does not mean the same."

The sharpest tension in the lives of the post-Feminist young comes from a workplace designed for people who can put in long, consecutive hours—mainly men and child-less women. Mothers, as well as many fathers, want jobs with more flexibility through job sharing, part-time hours, and leaves of absence. And they want the assurance that they can get back on the fast track when the demands of child-rearing ease off. More discussion and lobbying about these issues in the future is certain. Anne Crittenden, the author of *The Price of Motherhood*, has launched a lobbying group called MOTHER (Mothers Ought to Have Equal Rights), dedicated to promoting more family-friendly work-places, improved benefits for mothers, and a reduction of the "mommy tax."

Still, this tension can't be entirely, or even mostly, re-solved. The difficult truth is that the very economy that stirs the imaginations and ambitions of young people—that makes them work eighty hours a week in a start-up business, that makes them want to learn new skills or take on extra du-ties so they can get promoted or start their own businesses—is the same economy that will never be especially family-friendly and that often leaves even ambitious working mothers behind. Those who long for the Western European model, with its shorter workweeks, longer vacation times, and generous maternity and paternity leaves, fail to see that those more regulated economies also produce less excite-ment, less creativity, less opportunity, less money, less of what elsewhere I've called "ecstatic capitalism." Western

European workers don't work as hard; they also don't have as many opportunities to create new businesses, develop new skills, and get rich.

Many women seem to understand this reality. A number of those I interviewed said their crisis-driven jobs made part-time hours either impossible or a sure route to less interesting assignments. They did not blame their employers; they were quick to admit that if you tell clients that the person handling their case or account won't be in on Tuesdays, Wednesdays, and Fridays, you're going to lose them. All of the co-parenting fathers in Levine's book have had to give up not just Saturday golf but also dreams of writing a novel or of making partner. In such marriages, women are not the only ones who can't have it all. To these couples, everybody wins—Levine's male subjects appear pleased with how close they are to their children—but everybody loses too.

The more immediate point, however, is that while younger women are struggling with how to balance work and family, they have said goodbye to the radical dreams of feminism. Case in point: Rachel Foster, a Brooklyn mother of two young children who is on leave from her job as a Legal Aid lawyer. Foster is the great-granddaughter of William Z. Foster, the founder of the American Communist party, and his wife, Esther Peterson, a once well-known free-love nudist, who raised Rachel's grandfather in an anarchist community. She is the daughter of a social-worker mother who worked from the time Rachel was five weeks old. Foster expects to return eventually to "social justice and advocacy." But right now, as the largely content stay-at-home wife of a real-estate developer, one thing's for sure: she's not looking to live like her great-grandparents.

8

It's Morning After in America

SEX DOESN'T SELL: MISS PRIM IS IN. No, editors at the *New York Times* Sunday Styles section were not off their meds when they came up with that headline in early 2004. Just think about some of the Oscar nominees that year: there was *Seabiscuit*, a classic inspirational story of steadfast outsiders beating huge odds to win the race; *The Lord of the Rings: The Return of the King*, a mythic battle of good defeating evil, featuring female characters as pure as driven snow; *Master and Commander*, a nineteenth-century naval epic celebrating courage, discipline, and patriarchal authority. And then there was *Lost in Translation*, in which a man in the throes of a midlife crisis spends hours in a hotel room with a luscious young woman, and . . . they talk a lot.

If you listened carefully, you could hear something shifting deep beneath the manic surface of American culture. Rap stars had taken to wearing designer suits. Miranda Hobbes, *Sex and the City*'s redhead, had abandoned hooking up and a Manhattan co-op for a husband and a Brooklyn fixer-upper, where she helped tend her baby and ailing mother-in-law; even nympho Samantha had found a "meaningful relationship." Madonna was writing children's books. Gloria Steinem was an old married lady.

Yessiree, family values are hot! Capitalism is cool! Seven-grain bread is so yesterday, and red meat is back!

Wave away the colored smoke of the Jackson family circus, Paris Hilton, and the antics of San Francisco, and you can see how Americans have been self-correcting from a decades-long experiment with "alternative values." Slowly, almost imperceptibly during the 1990s, the culture began a lumbering, Titanic turn away from the iceberg, a movement reinforced by the 1990s economic boom and the shock of the 9/11 terrorist attacks. During the last ten years, most of the miserable trends in crime, divorce, illegitimacy, drug use, and the like that we saw in the decades after 1965 either turned around or stalled. Today Americans are consciously, deliberately embracing ideas about sex, marriage, children, and the American dream that are coalescing into a viable—though admittedly much altered—sort of bourgeois normality. What is emerging is a vital, optimistic, family-centered, entrepreneurial, and, yes, morally thoughtful citizenry.

To check a culture's pulse, first look at the kids, as good a crystal ball as we have. Yes, there's reason to worry: guns in the schools, drugs, binge drinking, cheating, Ritalin, gangs, bullies, depression, oral sex, Internet porn, you name it. Kids dress like streetwalkers and thugs, they're too fat, they don't read, they watch too much television, they never play outside, they can't pay attention, they curse like *South Park*'s Eric Cartman. The 1950s this ain't.

Yet marketers who plumb people's attitudes to predict trends are noticing something interesting about "Millennials," the term that generation researchers Neil Howe and William Strauss invented for the cohort of kids born between 1981 and 1999: they're looking more like Jimmy Stewart than James Dean. They adore their parents, they want to succeed, they're optimistic, trusting, cooperative, dutiful, and civic-minded. "They're going to 'rebel' by being, not worse, but better," write Howe and Strauss.

However counterintuitive, there's plenty of hard evidence to support this view. Consider the most basic indicator of social health: crime. The juvenile murder rate plummeted 70 percent between 1993 and 2001. By 2001 the arrest rate for all violent crime among juveniles was down 44 percent from its 1994 peak, reaching its lowest level since 1983. Juvenile arrests for burglary were also down 66 percent in that time period. Vandalism is at its lowest level in two decades. Despite all the headlines to the contrary, schools are a lot safer: school-based crimes dropped by close to half in the late 1990s. According to the Youth Risk Behavior Survey, the percentage of ninth- through twelfth-graders who reported being in a fight anywhere in the preceding twelve months dropped from 42 percent in 1991 to 33 percent in 2001, while those who had been in a fight on school property fell from 16 percent to 13 percent.

Something similar looks like it may be happening with adolescent drinking and drug use, on the rise throughout much of the nineties. Suddenly, around the turn of the millennium, the nation's teens began climbing back on the wagon. Monitoring the Future, an annual University of Michigan survey of the attitudes and behavior of high school students, reports that by 2002 the percentage of kids who reported binge drinking in the preceding thirty days was close to its lowest level in the twelve years that the survey has been following eighth- and tenth-graders and in the thirty years it has been following high school seniors. Although during the 1990s marijuana use rose sharply among eighth-graders and less dramatically among tenth- and twelfth-graders, by late in the decade the numbers began to fall. More broadly, the Department of Health and Human Services reports that all illicit teen drug use dropped 11 percent between 2001 and 2003. Ecstasy use, which soared between 1998 and 2001, fell by more than half among high schoolers. A 2003 National Center on Addiction and Substance Abuse study found that 56 percent of teenagers have no friends who drink regularly, up from 52 percent in 2002, and 68 percent say they have no friends using marijuana, up from 62 percent—even though 40 percent of them say they would have no trouble finding the stuff if they wanted it. They're just not interested.

And what about teen sex? Only yesterday you'd have thought there was no way to wrangle that horse back into the barn. No more. According to the Alan Guttmacher Institute, out-of-wedlock teen pregnancy rates have come down 28 percent from their high in 1990, from a peak of 117 per 1,000 girls ages fifteen to nineteen to 83.6 per 1,000 in 2000. The teen abortion rate also fell—by a third—during the same period. True, American kids still get pregnant at higher rates than those in other major Western nations, but the United States is the only country that saw a dramatic drop in teen pregnancy during the last decade.

While American kids are more often saying yes to birth control, even more of them, remarkably, are just saying no to sex, just as they are passing up marijuana and beer. According to the 1991 Youth Risk Behavior Survey, 54 percent of teens reported having had sex; a decade later the number was 46 percent. The number of high schoolers who reported four or more partners also fell from 18.7 percent to 14.2 percent.

Making the decline in sexual activity more striking is that it began just around the same time that Depo-Provera, a four-shots-a-year birth-control technology specifically aimed at teens, came on the market. It's often been said that the birth-control pill, which became available to the public in the early 1960s, propelled the sexual revolution. The lesson of Depo-Provera, which was accompanied by a decrease in sexual activity, is that it isn't technology that changes sexual behavior. It's the culture.

If you need more proof, check the surveys not just on kids' sexual behavior but on their attitudes toward sex. Millennials are notably more straitlaced than many of their let's-spend-the-night-together parents. American Freshman, an annual survey of more than a quarter of a million first-year kids at 413 four-year colleges, has found that young people have become less accepting of casual sex in the last 15 years. Between 1987 and 2001, those who agree with the statement "If two people really like each other, it's all right for them to have sex if they've known each other for a very short time" fell from 52 percent to 42 percent. Similarly, a recent National Campaign to Prevent Teen Pregnancy survey found that 92 percent of teenagers believe it is important for them "to get strong messages from society that they should not have sex until they are at least out of high school." Twenty-eight percent say they have become more opposed to teens having sex over the past several years, compared to 11 percent who say they are less opposed. It seems that it is adults who are skittish about abstinence, not kids: almost half the parents interviewed believe it is embarrassing for teens to admit they are virgins, yet only a quarter of teenagers think so.

Keep in mind that these beliefs do not exist in an isolated room of the teen brain marked "sex" or "pregnancy." They are part of a welter of attitudes and values that reinforce one another—a point lost on two front-page *New York Times* stories on the decline in teen pregnancy.

Determined to show that policies the *Times* does not approve of—especially welfare reform and abstinence education—did not affect the decline of adolescent childbearing, the paper missed the larger issue: these policies are both a result and a cause of a change in cultural beliefs percolating throughout American society, from the elites to the underclass. Fed up with the fallout from the reign of "if it feels good, do it"—not only as it played out in the inner city but in troubled middle-class families across the land— Americans are looking more favorably on old-fashioned virtues like caution, self-restraint, commitment, and personal responsibility. They are in the midst of a fundamental shift in the cultural zeitgeist that is driving so many seemingly independent trends in crime, sex, drugs, and alcohol in the same positive direction.

Look, for instance, at what's happening to teen alienation. If Millennials have a problem with authority, it's that they wish they had *more* of it. Poll after poll depicts a generation that thinks their parents are just grand. A 2003 *American Demographics* survey shows 67 percent of teens "give Mom an A." They tell interviewers for the National Campaign to Prevent Teen Pregnancy that they want *more* advice about sex from their parents. Summarizing opinion polls, researcher Neil Howe says this generation is at least as attached to their parents and their values as any generation before. "When it comes to 'Do you get along with your family?' it's never been as high. Same thing for 'Do you believe in the values of your parents?' When they're asked 'Do you trust your parents to help you with important life decisions?' they don't see parents as meddling or interfering," Howe concludes. "They're grateful."

In fact, when it comes to families, this generation is as mushy as a Hallmark card. A Harris Interactive survey of college seniors found that 81 percent planned to marry (12 percent already had) at a mean age of twenty-eight. Ninety-one percent hope to have children—and get this: on average, they'd like to have *three*. The 2001 Monitoring the Future survey found 88 percent of male high school seniors and 93 percent of females believing it is extremely or quite important to have a good marriage and family life. In a survey of college women conducted by the Institute for American Values, 83 percent said, "Being married is a very important goal for me." Over half the women surveyed said they would like to meet their husbands in college.

What makes this marriage schmaltziness so striking, of course, is that it's coming from people who grew up when that institution was in tatters. For a lot of culture watchers, nothing brings out the inner Cassandra more than the state of marriage—and for good reason, as we have seen, especially when you shift your focus from the young to the entire population. The proportion of never-married women between the ages of thirty and thirty-nine has almost tripled in the last thirty years. Laura Kipnis, author of the plaint *Against Love: A Polemic*, only seemed to be saying the obvious in her *New York Times* op-ed: "More and more people—heterosexuals that is—don't want to get or stay married these days, no matter their income level." After all,

Kipnis continued, quoting numbers that are a favorite of contemporary marriage "realists," "Only 56 percent of all adults are married, compared with 75 percent 30 years ago. The proportion of traditional married-couple-with-children American households has dropped to 26 percent of all households, from 45 percent in the early 1970's."

Except the obvious is wrong. Americans—particularly younger Americans at or approaching marriageable age— are marriage nuts. They meditate endlessly on the subject. Having put aside sitcoms about latte-drinking hook-up athletes—*Seinfeld* has died and gone to rerun heaven—they watch reality shows like *The Bachelor, The Bachelorette, The Littlest Groom, Average Joe,* and *Trista and Ryan's Wedding,* and movies like *My Big Fat Greek Wedding.* On *Friends* the space cadet Phoebe had a white-dress wedding while Monica and Chandler are married, adopting a baby, and moving to the burbs. In real life the number of married-couple families, after declining in the seventies and eighties, rose 5.7 percent in the nineties, according to demographer William H. Frey.

And in fact the incredible shrinking married-couple-with-children statistic cited by Kipnis is a statistical mirage, an artifact of two demographic trends unconnected with American attitudes toward knot tying. First, young people are marrying later; the average age is twenty-five for women, twenty-seven for men, up from twenty and twenty-three three decades ago. That means there are a lot more young singles out there than there were in 1970. Further swelling the ranks of these un–Ozzies and Harriets is the vastly increased number of empty nesters, retirees, and widows, beneficiaries of major health-care improvements over the past decades. There are 34 million Americans over sixty-five, and it's a safe bet that only those few living with their adult kids would be counted as part of a married-couple household with children. What it comes down to is that a smaller proportion of married couples with children is no more evidence of the decline of the family than more cars on the road is evidence of a decline in trucks.

Even on the fraught issue of out-of-wedlock births and divorce, there are grounds for hope. In the population at large, the decades-long trend toward family fragmentation has finally halted and, according to some numbers, is even reversing itself. Overall the proportion of children in married-parent families rose from 68 percent in 1998 to 69 percent in 2002—a tiny boost, to be sure, but the first upward tick in decades. More encouragingly, after plummeting between 1965 and 1992, the number of black children living with married parents rose from 34 percent in 1995 to 39 percent in 2000. Moreover the longitudinal Fragile Families and Child Wellbeing Study has found that half the poor, largely black, new mothers it surveys are living with the father at the time of their baby's birth.

Americans are even beginning to look at divorce with a more jaded eye. The divorce rate—statistically hard to pin down—is certainly stabilizing and possibly even declining from its record high of 50 percent. Not so long ago orthodox opinion would natter on about marital breakup as an opportunity for adults' "personal growth" or about "resilient children" who were "better off when their parents were happy." For the children of divorce who are now in their childbearing years, such sunny talk grates. They saw their mothers forced to move to one-bedroom apartments while their fathers went off with new girlfriends; they found out what it was like when your father moved from being the love object who read to you every night, to a guy who lives across the country whom you see once a year. When it comes to marriage and children, a lot of these damaged young adults are determined to do better. Nic Carothers, the eighteen-year-old son of divorced parents interviewed by the *Indianapolis Star*, explained his determination to avoid sex until he marries for life: "My father wasn't a very responsible man. I want to be a better father when the time is right." "I can't tell you how many thirtysomethings are still in therapy because of their parents' divorce," Catherine Stellin, of Youth Intelligence, told me. "Now we're hearing that maybe it's a good thing to stay together for the sake of the kids."

This change of view is not limited to the heartland. Writing in the mainstream *Atlantic Monthly*, Caitlin Flanagan offered mild praise for *The Proper Care and Feeding of Husbands*, by much reviled talk-show host Dr. Laura: "There are many of us who understand that once you have children, certain doors ought to be closed to you forever. That to do right by a child means more than buying the latest bicycle helmet and getting him on the best soccer team. . . . It means investing oneself completely in the marriage that wrought him." Flanagan went on to chastise feminist male-bashing. "Our culture is quick to point out the responsibilities husbands have to wives—they should help out with the housework, be better listeners, understand that a woman wants to be more than somebody's mother and somebody's wife—but very reluctant to suggest that a wife has a responsibility to a husband." Such views didn't sink Flanagan's career; she went on to publish her marriage-happy essays in the *bien-pensant New Yorker*.

In fact, applause for the nuclear family is now coming even from the American academy and from left-leaning advocacy groups. For decades, elites jeered at the assumption that changes in family structure would harm children; remember the guffaws that greeted Vice President Dan Quayle's pro-marriage *Murphy Brown* speech in 1992? But by the 1990s study after study began showing, as Barbara Dafoe Whitehead put it in a landmark 1993 *Atlantic Monthly* article, that "Dan Quayle Was Right"—that, on average, children in married, two-parent families do better than other kids by every measure of success. Once-skeptical experts began acknowledging that the traditionalists had it right all along, and advocates announced, in the words of ChildTrends, that "Marriage is one of the most beneficial resources for adults and children." Just a decade ago it seemed impossible to imagine a leftish organization like the Center for Law and Social Policy going on record that "society should try to help more children grow up with their two biological, married parents in a reasonably healthy, stable relationship," but that's what has happened.

Still not convinced there's anything to cheer about? Think about how much more child-centered Americans have become compared with fifteen or twenty years ago—the era of the latchkey kid, when the Nickelodeon children's network touted itself as a "parent-free zone" and *Home Alone* was the signature kids' movie. By the nineties, soccer moms had the keys to the house and the minivan, which was mounting up thousands of miles on trips to sports events, violin lessons, and swim meets. Studies showed a big drop in children's unstructured time. Even older kids came under their parents' hothouse scrutiny: "helicopter parents," in Neil Howe and William Strauss's term, hover over their children even after they leave for college, talking on the phone every day, visiting frequently, and helping them with their papers via e-mail.

The thirtysomethings who are today's young parents show every sign of keeping the hearth fires burning bright. According to *American Demographics*, Gen-X parents are "nostalgic for the childhood that boomers supposedly had. It's informed their model of the perfect, traditional marriage." As we've seen, Gen-X women are abandoning Ms. for Mrs.: according to a recent Harvard study, the past decade has seen a "substantial decrease" in the percentage of college-educated brides keeping their maiden names. If they can afford to, these Missuses are also choosing the nursery over the cubicle; by 2000 the number of women in the workforce with infants under one dropped from 59 percent to 55 percent, the first decline in decades. The *New York Times Magazine* has run high-profile stories of six-figure MBAs and lawyers leaving their jobs to be at home with their babies; *Time* published a cover story on the trend toward professional-class stay-at-homes; and *Cosmopolitan*, of all places, has found a new group of "housewife wannabes" who would like nothing more than to do a Donna Reed. And these young mothers want big families: *USA Today* reports that "the rate of women having more than two children rose steadily in the late 1990s."

Their traditionalism also embraces old-fashioned discipline. A 1999 Yankelovich survey found that 89 percent of Gen Xers think modern parents let kids get away with too much; 65 percent want to return to a more traditional sense of parental duty. "Character education" is hot in school districts across the country—as are the Girl Scouts, because, as official Courtney Shore told the *Washington Times*, "parents and communities are returning to values-based activities." Today's parenting magazines do a brisk trade in articles with titles like "Are You a Parent or a Pushover? Get a Discipline Makeover" and "Teaching Your Child Right from Wrong."

In the workplace as at home, these Gen Xers are powerhouses—hardworking and creative in the best American tradition. *Forbes* called them "the most entrepreneurial generation in American history." According to a study by Babson College professor Paul Reynolds, 80 percent of the 7 million strivers who started their own businesses in 1995 were between 19 and 31. Millennials look likely to continue the trend, with 56 percent of college seniors telling the Generation 2001 survey that they will likely work for themselves or start their own businesses. To meet the demand, reports *USA Today*, colleges offering entrepreneurship majors have soared from 175 to 500 since 1990.

All these more cautious, child-centered, and entrepreneurial values seem likely to translate into more conservative politics. According to the American Freshman survey, the number of first-year college students holding conservative political views grew from 14 percent to 21 percent between 1973 and 2003 while the percentage of liberals slumped from 1971's high of 38 percent to 24 percent. (The vast majority of college kids, like Americans in general, describe themselves as moderates.) Harvard's Institute of Politics shows 31 percent of young voters saying they are Republican, 27 percent Democrat, and 38 percent independent.

How could kids be going down a straight path at a time when their movies, TV, and music have been going over the edge, with reports by the Kaiser Family Foundation and the National Television Violence Study showing the sex and violence content of American entertainment exploding toxically over the last fifteen years? How could any culture flourish when the young spend their time watching *Victoria's Secret Fashion Show*, listening to Eminem, enacting the *Vagina Monologues* in a high school play (as they did recently at the Amherst, Massachusetts, Regional High School), and playing video games like "Suicide Bomber Game" or "Grand Theft Auto," where the player assumes the role of a coke dealer who rapes a prostitute? Yet researchers Howe and Strauss say that Millennials "are the first generation in living memory to be actually less violent, vulgar, and sexually charged than the popular culture adults are producing for them." How can that be?

Generational backlash counts for a lot: what we're seeing now is a rewrite of the boomer years. The truth is, Gen Xers and Millennials have some real gripes about the world their boomer parents constructed. When a 1999 Peter D. Hart Research Associates poll asked Americans between the ages of eighteen and thirty what experience had shaped their generation, the most common answer was "divorce and single-parent families." Growing up in the aftermath of America's great marriage meltdown, no wonder that young people put so much stock in marriage and family, their bedrock in the mobile twenty-first century.

In fact, in some respects young Gen-X adults resemble their Silent Generation grandparents more than their boomer parents, especially in their longing for suburban nesting as a dreamlike aspiration. On her blog "Church of the Masses," Gen Xer Barbara Nicolosi noted the explosion in the number of home-makeover shows like *Surprise by Design*, *Extreme Makeover: Home Edition*, and *Trading Spaces*. "For my generation, which has had to pay tens of thousands of dollars just to get educated—home ownership has become the American Dream again," she writes. "(For our boomer parents, who got to go to college for cheap and who mostly inherited property from their Greatest Generation parents, the American Dream seems to have been something about doing whatever they felt like without ever getting stuck or pregnant.)"

Then there is 9/11. Most trend spotters believe that Americans were already beginning to embrace more traditional values before the terrorist attacks: "September 11 accelerated a trend we had already seen," says Youth Intelligence veep Catherine Stellin. Soccer families went deeper into a cocooning mode; the heroic acts of police, firefighters, and soldiers doubtless encouraged the predisposition of Millennials to respect authority. In September 2001, the *Washington Post* reported, students at a Virginia progressive school—who choose their own courses, call teachers by their first names, and ignore a state law requiring them to say the Pledge of Allegiance—spontaneously began reciting the pledge at an assembly. The heartfelt patriotism and seriousness of the young has impressed even some cynical Bushwhacking lefties. Al Franken, author of the anti-Bush best-seller *Lies and the Lying Liars Who Tell Them*, was amazed to find that he "became irrationally attached" to U.S. soldiers—many of whom are young enough to be his children—during a Christmas USO trip to Iraq. "I got all teary-eyed at 'God Bless America,'" Franken wrote in the left-wing magazine *Mother Jones*. "In the front row I saw a black male soldier, swaying back and forth and really meaning it."

Also changing the zeitgeist is immigration. Marketers often characterize today's young generation by its "diversity"; a better way to put it is to say that it teems with immigrants and the sons and daughters of immigrants. Only 64 percent of Gen Xers and 62 percent of Millennials are non-Hispanic whites, compared with three-quarters of baby boomers. Twenty percent of today's teens have at least one immigrant parent. These kids often have a fervent work ethic—which can raise the bar for slacker American kids, as any high schooler with more than three Asian students in his algebra class will attest. Their parents tend toward traditionalism when it comes to marriage and family, with minuscule divorce and illegitimacy rates among Asians (though not among Hispanics, where families headed by a single mother have expanded rapidly). Immigrant kids are more likely to listen to their parents, and they tend not to be alienated ingrates who take their country's prosperity and opportunities for granted. As a Vietnamese high schooler wrote on Pop-Politics.com: "When your parents have traveled thousands of miles to live here, when they spend three hours a day driving you and your siblings to various activities, when they paid hundreds of thousands of dollars for a cramped house they could have bought half-price elsewhere, you feel a debt."

And that drive and seriousness take us to reason number four: the information economy. According to the American Freshman survey, 73.8 percent of college kids say succeeding financially is an important life goal—a huge rise from the 40 percent who thought so in the late 1960s. These kids know they have to be hardworking, forward-looking, and pragmatic. But they know opportunity is out there, having recently witnessed one of the most remarkable booms in American history, a time when black family poverty fell from 44 percent in 1992 to 23 percent in 1999, and when an astonishing 23 percent of households began earning more than $75,000 a year. Although plenty of Gen Xers lost their shirts when the dot-com bubble burst in 2000, there's little sign they are souring on the free market. J. Walker Smith, president of the Yankelovich consultancy group, told *Adweek* that Gen Xers "feel more comfortable than boomers in reinventing themselves—they're more self-reliant and more self-directed. They're at home in an uncertain market and are going to look for a way to reengineer opportunities for themselves right here."

Some argue that we are witnessing the rise of a shallow, money-grubbing generation. After all, the number of kids who say "developing a meaningful philosophy of life" is an important goal has plummeted during the same period in which the number of those valuing financial success has soared. But remember: living in an age of "ecstatic capitalism," middle-class young people, who often have had opportunities to hone their talents in everything from computer science to theater to debate, expect work to be gratifying as well as remunerative. They see work itself as a source of meaning as well as an engine of self-discipline.

Comfort with the advanced market economy also helps explain how it is that a vulgar popular culture has not had the corrupting influence on behavior that we might have feared. Growing up steeped in entertainment media, the young learn early on to be skeptical toward its blandishments. They don't believe they take their ideas about how to live a decent life from *Dawson's Creek* or 50 Cent. In a recent survey from the National Campaign to Prevent Teen Pregnancy, for instance, teens were asked who influences their values about sex: only 4 percent answered "the media" while 45 percent answered "my parents." Of course kids don't necessarily know where they're getting their ideas.

And of course popular culture has *some* influence on their behavior. Presumably suburban middle-school boys who grab and fondle girls in the halls, while the girls hint at their availability for oral sex, did not learn any of this at the dinner table.

Even after all these changes, we still live in a post–sexual-revolution culture. Nobody pretends we're going back to the 1950s. Americans may have abandoned the credo of "if it feels good, do it," but they still embrace sexual pleasure as a great human good and take pride in advertising their own potential for success in that area. David Brooks coined the term "bobo" to refer to bourgeois bohemians, but the newest generation of bobos might be better described as bourgeois booty-shakers. Young mothers go to "strip aerobics" classes, where they do their workout by pole dancing, before they go off to pick up little Tiffany at kindergarten. Madonna does some provocative tongue wrestling with Britney Spears on national television, but everyone knows that in reality she glories in being a Hollywood soccer mom (and Mrs. Guy Ritchie, as she would have it). An edgy exterior no longer necessarily connotes a radical lifestyle: not long ago I watched a heavily pierced couple as the bride-to-be, with her stringy, dyed red hair, torn jeans, and bright green sneakers, squealed over the pear-shaped diamond engagement ring she was trying on. Go figure.

The popular media has been trying to make sense of these crosscurrents. Some writers seem to grasp that they can bombard their viewers with breast and fart jokes, but in the end people are still interested in how to live meaningful lives. Consider the WB network's popular series *Gilmore Girls*. The main character, Lorelai Gilmore, is a single thirtysomething who had a baby when she was sixteen. A motormouthed girl-woman, she picks fights with her now-teenage daughter over the size of their "boobs," makes pop-culture allusions as obsessively as any teenybopper, and mugs and pouts during her weekly adolescent-style tiffs with her own parents. The daughter, Rory, on the other hand, is the proto-Millennial: sober, hardworking, respectful, and chaste. In an early episode, her hell-raiser mother's jaw drops when she hears that her daughter hasn't really thought about having sex with her boyfriend. Meanwhile Rory becomes a freshman at Yale, where she writes for the school paper and reads, you know, literature. (*The Sun Also Rises?* On the network that gave us *Dawson's Creek?*) Yes, this is a piece of pop-culture effluvium, but its point, made weekly, is that Rory has the promising future while her mother reflects the childish past.

Look also at *American Wedding*, the sequel to *American Pie*, a foul teen cult film about a group of high school boys determined to have sex before they graduate. (On second thought, don't—unless your idea of cinematic fun includes extended jokes about pubic hair and dog doo.) In one scene of the sequel, which depicts the nuptials of one of the couples that we met in the earlier movie, the bride-to-be, Michelle, asks her future father-in-law to help her write her vows. "How do you describe making love?" he asks her, to get her started on her composition. But Michelle can only think of vulgarisms: she stands for a generation that, like Shakespeare's Caliban, has yet to be taught a civilized language. Still, her wedding, complete with white gown, bridesmaids, toasts, and a band that plays fox-trots, clearly reflects her longing for the sort of refined feelings that she has no words for. "How did a perv like you become such a great guy?" Michelle asks her new husband, after she delivers her vows, marked by their sincerity if not their poetry, during "the wedding of her dreams." "How did a nympho like you become such a great girl?" he asks her in turn. It is a wonder.

And that surprise takes us back to the most vexing issue of our day: gay marriage, which encapsulates the tension between the sexual revolution and the new conventionality. On the one hand, it asserts the value of unrestricted sexual desire; on the other, it celebrates our new seriousness about constructing traditional meaning, solidity, and connection out of those desires in a vulgar and rootless postliberation landscape. Regardless of how Americans resolve this tension, the change in the cultural zeitgeist means that, for all their wealth and fame, the Quentin Tarantinos and Ice Ts of this culture do not own it. The public has its own mind, influenced by forces more powerful than the television or movie screen. The purveyors of fashion and entertainment try to decipher the cultural mood.

So recent ads for Gucci leave sexual decadence behind for mystery and romance. Why? Because these trendsetters sense something new. "What we did was sort of instinctual. We just felt there was something in the air," Doug Lloyd, one of Gucci's admen, told the *New York Times*. "Believe it or not, I am a little sick of blatant sexual poses in advertising," Gucci designer Tom Ford, a man who once had a G shaved into a model's crotch and hired a photographer to snap the results, told *Harper's Bazaar*. So Abercrombie and Fitch canceled its Christmas catalog after the outcry over its orgy tips for teens. So Viacom president Mel Karmazin chided his radio stations: "This company won't be a poster child for indecency." More surprising than Janet Jackson's breast reveal was the vigorous public spanking that she and Justin Timberlake received after it was over. For what it's worth, my sixteen-year-old daughter tells me that the girls she knows with pierced navels now see them as "skanky" and wish they could undo them. Now they care about SEXY TOPS THAT DON'T LOOK TRASHY, as a *Seventeen* headline promised to explain to its teen readers.

With their genius for problem solving and compromise, pragmatic Americans have seen the damage that their decades-long fling with the sexual revolution and the transvaluation of traditional values wrought. And now, without giving up the real gains, they are earnestly knitting up their unraveled culture. For some Americans, it is a moment of tremendous promise.

Index

Index

American family (*continued*)
of, 36; and soccer moms,
157
American Freshman survey, 151
American Law Institute, 43
American marriage, 13, 32, 44;
American principles, as
reflection of, 34, 35;
characteristics of, 5, 6; as
child-centered, 7–8; and
divorce, 42; and poor, 11;
transformation of, 42
American mothers: education
levels of, 18
American Pie (film), 165
American Revolution: and self-
determination, 35
American Society for
Reproductive Medicine, 140
American Wedding (film), 165
America Works, 93
Anderson, Elijah, 113, 114
Andrews, D. J., 91, 92, 93
Angelou, Maya, 73
Angier, Natalie, 143
Annie E. Casey Foundation, 65
Asians, 162; teen pregnancy
rate, as lowest, 122
Auletta, Ken, 67, 68
Austen, Jane, 34

Baltimore Sun: black family
series in, 67
Barton, Lorraine, 115
Belkin, Lisa, 137
Benzino, Ray, 91
Berger, Brigitte, 82
Beyond the Melting Pot (Glazer
and Moynihan), 54
Billingsley, Andrew, 58, 59
Binge drinking: decline in,
149–150

Birth control pills, 16; and
Depo-Provera, 151
Black children: and education,
74; and poverty, 73–74;
rearing of, 78, 79, 80
Black Entertainment Television
(BET) network, 89
Black Families in White America
(Billingsley), 58
Black males: drift, sense of in,
107; incarceration of, 90,
104; life script, lack of, 105;
and manhood, 100, 101,
112, 113; as marriage risk,
104; mistrust of, 102; sons,
relationships with, 105;
unemployment of, 90
Black music: father loss, as
theme in, 92
Black Student Achievement
(Sampson), 86
Blustain, Sarah, 135
Boomer generation, 161;
generational backlash
against, 160; and
immigration, 162
Bourgeois bohemians, 164
Brennan, William, 61
Brodie, Janet, 36
Brontë, Charlotte, 34
Brooks, David, 164
Brooks-Gunn, Jeanne, 77, 86
Brown v. Board of Education, 52,
72
Brown, Taisha, 109, 110, 119
Brownmiller, Susan, 137
Burkam, David, 87
Bush administration, 70
Bush, George W., 126
Bushnell, Horace, 37
Bust (Internet magazine),
136

Index

Index

Index

Index

Index

human universal, 5; inner city, disappearance of in, 125; legal system, attitude toward, 7; as love-match, 34; as minimalist institution, 42; as optional, 30; reforming of, 43–44; and self-government, 33; as social institution, 29; and spirituality, 33; suburbia, comeback of in, 125; working-class communities, fading of in, 125; and young women, 129

Marriage Gap, 21, 23, 25, 30; and caste society, 26; implications of, on children, 22; as self-perpetuating, 26; social divide of, 22

Marriage, a History: From Obedience to Intimacy, or How Love Conquered Marriage (Coontz), 61

Marriage market theory, 104; and jobs, 107

Marryat, Frederick, 38

Marsh, Katherine, 134

Massachusetts: marriage in, 39

Master and Commander (film), 147

McKissick, Floyd, 56

McLanahan, Sara, 22, 23, 68, 69

Mead, Lawrence, 66, 68

Meaningful Differences (Hart and Risley), 79

Middle-class families, 4, 5; child rearing of, 81, 82; life script of, 49, 109

Millennial generation, 148–149; authority, respect for, 152, 161; and boomers, 160; as entrepreneurial, 159; and

immigration, 162; as marriage nuts, 154; as straitlaced, 151, 160; work, as source of meaning, 163

Millner, Denene, 98, 105

Mincy, Ron, 91

Minority teens: life script, lack of, 109, 110; marriage, as irrelevant, 110. *See also* Underclass.

Miscegenation laws, 44

The Mission, 86; children, nurturing of, 25, 82; as expensive, 85; happiness, pursuit of, 83; middle-class, as dedicated to, 25; and poor parents, 85, 87

Monitoring the Future, 149, 153

Montana, 117

Moore v. City of East Cleveland, 61

Morrison, Toni, 60

MOTHER (Mothers Ought to Have Equal Rights), 145

Motherhood, and feminism, 139, 141, 142; and the Mission, 25; and underclass, 117, 119. *See also* Single mothers.

Motherhood Report, The, 144

Mother's Book (Child), 37

Moyers, Bill, 67

Moynihan, Daniel Patrick, 6–7, 49, 51, 53–56, 58, 62, 69; as prophetic, 67; racism, accusations of, 7

Moynihan Report, 52, 67, 68, 89; attacks on, 57; lesson of, 71; as racist, charges of, 56

Ms. Foundation for Women, 127

Murphy Brown (television series), 157

Index

Index

Index

Index

A NOTE ON THE AUTHOR

Kay S. Hymowitz is a senior fellow at the Manhattan Institute in New York City and a contributing editor of *City Journal*. Born in Philadelphia, she studied at Brandeis, Tufts, and Columbia universities; before turning to writing full time, she taught English literature and composition at Brooklyn College and the Parsons School of Design. Ms. Hymowitz has written extensively on education and childhood in America, in articles for the *New York Times*, the *Washington Post*, the *Wall Street Journal*, the *New Republic*, the *Public Interest, Commentary, Dissent*, and *Tikkun*, among other publications. Her books include *Liberation's Children: Parents and Kids in a Postmodern Age* and *Ready or Not: Why Treating Our Children as Small Adults Endangers Their Future and Ours*. She lives in Brooklyn with her husband and three children.